Spitfir

over

Sussex

The exploits of 602 Squadron

To Roger Best With my Wishes

David Rowland

FP
Finsbury Publishing

This book is dedicated to the 602 pilots who flew from a small field at Westhampnett and were part of a much larger unit who fought and won the Battle of Britain during the summer of 1940.

First published 2000; new expanded edition 2011

By the same author:
The Brighton Blitz
The Coastal Blitz
Target Brighton
War in the City 1 and 2
Survivors

David Rowland was four when war broke out in September 1939. He still has vivid memories of the night when Brighton burned, of sleeping in a Morrison shelter, of carrying a gas mask and of the many evacuations from the classroom to the surface air raid shelters in Finsbury Road, outside his school.

Throughout the war years he lived in a terraced house in Grove Street, Brighton, an area of which he is fiercely proud. On two occasions bombs fell within a few hundred yards of his home.

He attended two schools in Brighton before working for Sainsbury's in 1950. He left in 1958 to join the Brighton Borough Police, where he served until a medical discharge in 1985.

Cover illustration: Dugald Cameron.

British Library Cataloguing-in Publication Data.
A catalogue record for this book is available from the British Library.

ISBN 978-0-9558037-0-3

Published by Finsbury Publishing, 2 Harvest Close, Telscombe Cliffs, Peacehaven, East Sussex BN10 7JG

Printed by 4 Edge, 7A Eldon Way, Hockley, Essex SS5 4AD

Introduction

I was looking through some wartime books about the Battle of Britain and a picture in one of them quickly drew my attention. It showed a pilot in flying uniform being brought ashore in a small fishing boat and being landed at Bognor Regis in West Sussex. It transpired that the pilot had been shot down in flames while in combat with a German fighter and had baled out.

I later saw another interesting picture and that was of a Spitfire lying on its back in a field at Iford, near Lewes, East Sussex. This had crash-landed after being in combat.

I soon realised that in both cases the pilot was Sergeant Cyril Babbage, who was a member of 602 (City of Glasgow) Squadron and based at Westhampnett. I knew nothing about 602 Squadron, but the pilot interested me and so I decided to discover something about them both.

There was to be a very big surprise awaiting me. Not only had the pilot survived the war, but 602 turned out to be one of the top fighter squadrons with a wonderful history that was splashed with acts of tremendous bravery.

The two Babbage pictures. The crashed Spitfire was, amazingly, repairable.

At this stage I had only a few books to refer to, but my appetite was whetted. I first wrote to RAF Innsworth and they put me in touch with an ex-wartime Spitfire pilot who just happened to have served with 602 Squadron during the summer of 1940. I couldn't believe my luck, and very soon we were writing to each other. He was one of the characters of 602, Glen 'Nuts' Niven. I wrote other letters to RAF Innsworth and was alerted to other members of the Squadron, including the commanding officer, 'Sandy' Johnstone. I managed to be put in touch with a few more members, including one as far away as Australia.

Each and every one offered help, and my information gradually grew. I was very lucky to make contact with Douglas McRoberts who had researched the squadron some years earlier and published a book which is generally accepted as the definitive book about its history. 'Lions Rampant', however, had been long out of print.

A number of other books have been written about 602, but I thought I would like to write one telling the story of their exploits in Sussex sixty years ago.

I have recorded their wartime stories and they have been kind enough to check them for me. I am particularly pleased to have made the acquaintance of these marvellous and brave men who, some of them in their early 20s, risked their lives several times a day to save our country.

The book includes the stories of Flight Lieutenant Dunlop Urie, who had the distinction of wrecking a brand new Spitfire in just minutes; of Flying Officer

A German Bf109 on display 'somewhere on the south coast'. These aircraft were used to entice the public to put money into the Spitfire funds.

Donald Jack, who was very often in the thick of things, with 'Nuts' Niven acting as his wingman; and of one of the youngest pilots of the time, Pilot Officer Paddy Barthropp, who had a remarkably incident-packed war. He not only fought in the Battle of Britain, acting on many occasions as a 'Tail end Charlie' - one of the most dangerous positions in formation flying - but in 1942 he was shot down over France, becoming a prisoner of war. He was assigned to Stalag

Luft III, the camp made famous by the film *The Great Escape*. He was in one of the huts ready to take his turn, but after 76 men had escaped from the camp they were rumbled by the German guards.

I was to uncover many facts about these young pilots and about the

Whoops! A nose landing for Alastair Grant in January, 1940 on the icy ground at the squadron's Drem headquarters.

King George VI shakes hands with Squadron Leader Sandy Johnstone while inspecting 602 Squadron in 1940.

squadron itself. They had many 'firsts', such as flying over Mount Everest, shooting down the first German bomber on British soil and attacking and seriously wounding Rommel in Normandy prior to D-Day. They were the second highest scoring unit and suffered the least pilot loss, a true reflection on their skill and endeavour.

However, the highlight for me has been the invitation to become an associate member of 602 Squadron Museum and to be linked to these ex-wartime Spitfire pilots. I am so proud to have had the opportunity to converse with these brave men, now in their 80s, some not now enjoying the best of health. I hope and pray that through these pages they will never be forgotten.

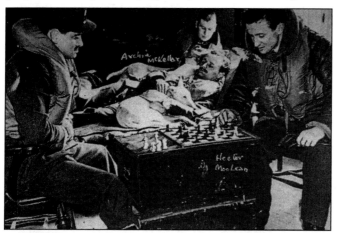

Tactical formations. Members of the squadron relaxing with a game of chess at their Westhampnett base.

What the initials mean . . .

ADU	Aircraft Delivery Unit	DSO	Distinguished Service Order
AFC	Air Force Cross	E&RFTS	Elementary & Reserve Flying Training School
AFTS	Advanced Flying Training School	FTS	Flying Training School
AI	Airborne Interception	ITW	Initial Training Wing
AOC	Air Officer Commanding	OTU	Operational Training Unit
CB	Companion of the Order of the Bath	RAAF	Royal Australian Air Force
		RAFO	Reserve of Air Force Officers
CO	Commanding Officer	RAFVR	Royal Air Force Volunteer Reserve
DFC	Distinguished Flying Cross		
DFM	Distinguished Flying Medal	RCAF	Royal Canadian Air Force
		SASO	Senior Air Staff Officer

602 Squadron, 1925–1957

*T*he Auxiliary Air Force was the brainchild of Sir Hugh Trenchard, whose vision was of a *'Corps d'elite* of mechanical yeomanry' - an airborne version of the Territorial Army. The vision became reality in 1925, and on September 12 the adjutant, Flight Lieutenant 'Dan' Martyn, RAF, arrived at Renfrew - the 'Moorpark' aerodrome - and 602 (City of Glasgow) Squadron was close to becoming born.

Two days later the first commanding cfficer arrived (Squadron Leader C.N.Lowe MC, DFC and RAF) and the following day 602 was officially formed as a light bomber squadron. It became the first to fly, a month ahead of the London and Edinburgh squadrons. The men insisted on wearing the 'Tartan' with their dress uniforms, eventually winning official approval to wear the 'Grey Douglas'- courtesy of the Duke of Hamilton, who had sons in both 602 and 603 Squadrons.

They were ordered by the top brass to come up with a suitable Squadron Crest. It is claimed, with tongue in cheek, that a lot of thought went into the design. The initial motif was 'a bowler hat with crossed umbrellas', the motto being 'City of Glasgow (Gentleman's) Bomber Squadron'

The top brass, with a sigh and total exasperation, told them to take things more seriously and to devise something more in keeping with the situation. The boys of the squadron, with suitably serious faces, then came up with a lion rampant superimposed on the St. Andrew's Cross, adding the impressive Latin motto *Cave Leonem Cruciatum*, which they interpreted as 'Beware the Lion when crossed'.

Once the new emblem was given royal assent by the King, the squadron wags claimed that the true Latin translation was, 'Beware the castrated Lion'. As one of the chief perpetrators, solicitor Dunlop Urie, said: 'Sounds like good advice.'

The 602 badge. Latinists in the squadron had some fun with it.

Many of the pilots would go on to greater things. George Pinkerton was the first auxiliary to command a regular fighter squadron and later took control of the Merchant Ship Fighter Unit, which catapulted Hurricanes off specially converted ships in the defence of vital Atlantic convoys.

Sandy Johnstone, the commanding officer during the Battle of Britain, would go on to lead a Spitfire wing in the defence of Malta.

Dunlop Urie, after recovering from serious leg injuries sustained in August 1940, would lead the first British Fighter Unit in Russia, while Andy McDowall, the squadron's 'hard man', would emerge as one of the Battle of Britain's top scorers and then go on to command the RAF's first Jet Fighter Squadron in 1944.

Archie McKellar, from Paisley, only 5'3" and full of high spirits as well as supreme skills, would become the top scoring RAF pilot in the Battle of Britain, being awarded two DFC's and a DSO in just two frantic months defending London.

Then there was Findlay Boyd, a coal-master's son from Thornton Hall, destined to become one of the RAF's top fighter pilots of the war. He had a nose for trouble and hated the enemy. Later on in the war, while commanding Kenley Spitfire Wing, he stumbled across the German Battle-cruiser, *Scharnhorst* making a break for home through the English Channel and promptly attacked it at mast height level through a curtain of fire. He ended the war as a Group Captain with 21 enemy aircraft to his credit.

Some 14 of Fighter Command's 62 squadrons during the Battle of Britain were AAF units and were responsible for the destruction of a third of the German aircraft shot down.

The squadron began flying DH9A's from Moorpark aerodrome at Renfrew in Scotland. It was originally a bomber squadron but converted to fighters a few months before the

Pint-sized hero: Archie McKellar of 602 was the top-scoring RAF pilot in the Battle of Britain.

outbreak of the second world war, in May 1939. The squadron was finally disbanded in 1957, but during those 32 years it won many top honours as well as a number of 'firsts'

Two of its pilots, the Marquis of Douglas and Clydesdale (later the Duke of Hamilton) and Flight lieutenant David McIntyre, were the first men to fly over Mount Everest.

602 were the first Auxiliary Squadron to be equipped with Spitfires - they were delivered on the May 8, 1939 - becoming only the seventh squadron in the whole of the Royal Air Force to have them.

On August 24 they were embodied into the Royal Air Force in anticipation of the outbreak of war. At this stage they were commanded by Squadron Leader Douglas Farquhar at RAF Abbotsinch, with a total strength of 22 Officers and 174 airmen.

With the Spitfires, they were involved in the shooting down of the very first German bomber, on Monday, October 16, 1939, by Flt Lt George Pinkerton. This aircraft, a Junkers Ju 88, crashed in the Firth of Forth, the pilot being captured and pulled from the sea unconscious, minutes from death. Pinkerton, a farmer, had for his wingman (No. 2) Archie McKellar, and their guns shot out the engines of the Junkers Ju 88. It has long been a source of argument as to whether it was 602 or 603 (City of Edinburgh) Squadron who actually got the first 'kill' of the war, but contemporary reports strongly support Pinkerton's claim.

This incident marked the start of what was to be an unparalleled contribution by the 'week-end flyers' of the Scottish fighter squadron of the Auxiliary Air Force - accountants, lawyers, farmers and bankers - to Britain's war in the air.

The two Scottish squadrons were together when the Germans tried their hardest to attack Britain - by the back door. These early skirmishes were to stand them in good stead the following summer when they were in southern England playing a critical role in the Battle of Britain.

They were also involved in shooting down the first German aircraft to crash on British soil (rather than into the sea) during the second world war. A Heinkel He 111 landed at Long Newton's Farm, Humbie, near Edinburgh on Saturday October 28, 1939. Two crewmen were captured and two others killed.

In August 1940, the squadron moved southwards from Scotland to a small airfield at Westhampnett, West Sussex, a satellite airfield of Tangmere. It was very soon involved in the Battle of Britain and, due to the skill of their pilots, they soon established themselves as one of the leading squadrons, finishing the conflict with the second highest total of 'kills'. They also boasted the lowest total of 'pilot loss rate' as well as being the longest serving squadron in the front line.

The squadron was withdrawn back to Scotland towards the end of December 1940. It then served spells at Prestwick and Ayr when Spitfire II's were received in May 1941, and in July returned south to Kenley ,taking on Mark Vb's for cross-Channel operations which continued throughout the year.

Early days: A wonderful painting by Dugald Cameron of DH9As and Avro 505 above Renfrew in 1926. [Dugald Cameron]

602 Pilots during the Battle of Britain

[Taken from a letter to the Lord Provost of Glasgow by the father of Hector Maclean, dated January 24, 1941]

Sq Ldr. A V R Johnstone
(Commanding Officer)
Flt Lt. J D Urie
('A' Flight Commander)
Flt Lt. R F Boyd
('B' Flight Commander)
Fg Off. C J Mount
('A' Flight Commander-
after Flt Lt J D Urie)
Plt Off. E W Aries
Sgt. C F Babbage
Fg Off. P C C Barthropp
Sgt. Bracton
Fg Off. W H Coverley - (killed
in action*)
Sgt. A W Eade.
Plt Off. A L Edy - (killed in
action)
Sgt. D W Elcombe - (killed in
action*)
Fg Off. P J Ferguson
Plt Off. G Fisher
Plt Off. D H Gage - (killed in
action.)
Flt Sgt. J Gillies - (killed in
action.)
Plt Off. O V Hanbury - (killed
in action.)
Fg Off. J S Hart
Plt Off. W P Hopkin
Plt Off. D M Jack

Plt Off. A Lyall - (killed in
action.)
Fg Off. C H Maclean
Sgt. A McDowall
Plt Off. H W Moody - (killed in
action*)
Plt Off. H G Niven.
Plt Off. R A Payne- (killed in
action)
Sgt. J Proctor
Plt Off. T G F Ritchie - (killed
in action)
Plt Off. S N Rose
Sgt. W B Smith
Sgt. M H Sprague - (killed in
action*)
Fg Off. P C Webb
Sgt. B E P Whall - (killed in
action*)
Sgt. G A Whipps - (killed in
action)

(Plus probably Sgt. L S Smith for a short period.)

Abbreviations:-
Sq Ldr. - Squadron Leader.
Flt Lt. - Flight Lieutenant.
Fg Off. - Flying Officer.
Plt Off. - Pilot Officer.
Flt Sgt. - Flight Sergeant.
Sgt. - Sergeant.

* killed during the Battle of
Britain.

In July 1942 the unit moved to Peterhead in the north of Scotland, before again coming south - this time to Biggin Hill in mid August to take part in the ill fated Dieppe Raid on August 19. They were at Biggin Hill for only a short while, returning to Peterhead until January 1943. They then again came south, this time to Perranporth in Cornwall, which provided a new area of operations. During that summer they had a number of bases, including Lasham, Fairlop and Bognor.

They moved to Newchurch and then in October to Detling, where they were issued with Spitfire IXb's. They had to give these new aircraft up when they again returned to Scotland and, in the Orkneys, they had to take over the Mark Vb's. March saw them return to Detling and again have the IXb's, becoming part of 125 wings, 2nd TAF. Pre-invasion work began at once, and in April the unit moved to Ford.

The invasion of Europe was covered from here from June 6, 1944, the wing moving to France on the 25th. In August, as the breakout from Normandy began, Mark IX's took over from the IXb's and then by mid-September the unit found themselves in Belgium. However, by the end of that month all its squadrons were sent back to England to join ADGB, making way for Spitfire XIV units. Re-equipped with IXb's again at Coltishall, the squadron moved to Matlask to undertake bomber escort duties.

About the end of the year Spitfire XVI's arrived, coinciding with a move to Swannington, and then Mustangs took over the escort work. The Squadron began dive-bombing attacks on V2 launching sites and other prime targets. During 1945, as the war came to an end, the unit were based at Ludham and Coltishall and little action was recorded.

A little light relief: Padre Sutherland with the great Harry Lauder at Drem, just before 602 left for Westhampnett.

The code letters 'LO' were carried throughout the war.

602 Squadron was the fighter squadron that many pilots wanted to join, and the successors to the original 'Glasgow Boys' included some very famous names. It is quite incredible that eight of the RAF's 40 top scoring pilots flew

with 602. Top Aces like Al (Nine Lives) Deere, softly spoken 'Paddy' Finucane and 'Ginger' Lacey, who shot down the Heinkel that bombed Buckingham Palace - and who later stood King George VI a beer in 602's mess.

Then there was South African Chris Le Roux, under whose leadership 602 shot up Rommel's car, wounding him so seriously that it put him out of the war.

There were three Frenchmen: Pierre Clostermann (probably the most famous); Jacques Remlinger, whose cavalier approach to life on the ground was almost matched by his exploits in the air; and their commander, Pierre Aubertin, who openly wept in the cockpit of his 602 Spitfire when flying close escort over the Allied forces on D-Day as they landed on French soil.

Max Sutherland, the man known as 'The Boss', was a veteran fighter pilot and natural leader. He was a boxing champion and became comanding officer of the squadron just as they were preparing for their most epic operation of the war. He also found himself in charge of some of the world's most experienced and battle-hardened fighter pilots.

Writing in his diary the night after he led the Squadron over the D-Day beaches, he wrote`: 'I was able to put a team of 12 pilots into the air with a total number of operational sorties of 2,000, which averaged 166 per man. No other squadron that has such an experienced team will ever fly together again in the future.' None ever has.

Under the 'Boss's leadership, and with Raymond Baxter (of BBC fame) as his senior flight commander, 602 did things with their Spitfires that nobody else could possibly achieve. Pinpoint dive-bombing attacks on V1 flying bomb sites in 1944 were followed by attacks on V2 sites.

During one of these attacks Tommy 'Cupid' Love, was startled to see one of these massive bombs suddenly rise up from its launching base just as he started his low level attack. He took careful aim and fired his 20mm cannons. This was almost certainly the first, and possibly the only, time that an attempt was made to destroy a V2 in flight.

Baxter later said: 'Thank God he didn't hit it, or we'd all have been blown to smithereens.'

In March 1945, Sutherland and Baxter led 602 on the war's most remarkable pinpoint raid. Six Spitfires crossed the North Sea at low level, flying in line abreast at less than 30 feet under radar cover. They flew over The Hague, barely ten feet above the rooftops, through a barrage of flak and small arms fire. Their target was the Gestapo headquarters in the Bataasher-Mex building, which was closely flanked by a church on one side and civilian tenements on the other.

With their speed a little over 300mph, the six Spitfires dropped down over a wall, took out the second floor windows with their cannons and then threw their 250-pound bombs through the shattered frames. Just 11 seconds later the bombs exploded: the neighbouring buildings remained intact, but the German HQ was a ruin. The six Spitfires made it safely to an advanced Allied base at Ursel, a job exceedingly well done. (These days we take these low-level attacks in our stride, but this attack more than 50 years ago was truly remarkable.)

Sutherland had earlier made a promise to Glasgow's provost, 'Paddy' Dollan, that he would carry the City of Glasgow crest to the very heart of Germany. A few weeks later, with the war in Europe won, he was detailed to command the RAF fighters escorting Winston Churchill's aircraft to the Potsdam Peace Conference. As they approached Berlin, people on the ground were amazed to see the fighter leader peel off. As the brand new Mustang screamed down the sky towards the city centre, the people half-expected to be fired upon. Max Sutherland's aircraft flew straight down the centre of Wilhelmstrasse, about 40 feet off the ground, the freshly painted 'Lion Rampant' clear for all to see. He had kept his promise.

Archie McKellar, who had been involved in the very first downing of a German aircraft way back in October 1939, made a classic remark when he found out that war had been declared. 'Christ,' he said 'I joined for the dancing , not the fighting.' Sadly, he wouldn't see the end of it: early on the morning of Friday November 1, 1940, he volunteered to stand in for one of his young pilots, just back from leave. Within an hour of take off he was dead, shot down over Kent by a Bf. 109 - for once, one he didn't see.

The squadron was disbanded on May15, 1945, by which time they were credited with the destruction of 150 enemy aircraft.

After the war had finished, 602 Squadron was reformed in its auxiliary state, flying Spitfires from Abbotsinch (now Glasgow airport) and, for a time, Renfrew. In January 1951 the Spitfires gave way to Vampire jet aircraft: these were flown until the final disbandment in January 1957.

During the squadron's 32 years many young brave pilots flew with it. During the Battle of Britain its success can only be described as outstanding. Apart from

This is a Spit XVI which I flew on several Ops with 602 (TB 382)
Raymond Baxter

Spitfire L.F. XVIe   602 (City of Glasgow) Squadro

Raymond Baxter, who became a BBC personality, signed this card: 'This is a Spit XVI which I flew on several Ops with 602 (TB 382).'

being the longest serving squadron in the front line, recording the second highest total of 'kills' and the lowest pilot loss rate, it was awarded more than a dozen DFCs. Among its ranks was the RAF's top scorer during the Battle of Britain, Flying Officer Archie McKellar, DSO, DFC and bar. His total was 17 'kills' and another three shared, as well as five probables and three damaged - some achievement.

As the war years progressed the squadron started to become 'international'. Pilot Officer Glen 'Nuts Niven, who flew throughout the Battle of Britain, had been a lone Canadian: now there were not only more Canadians, but pilots from Australia, New Zealand, Poland and even a member of the Free French.

Of the five pilots who were killed during the Battle of Britain, two are remembered on the Runnymede Memorial panel, while the other three are buried in cemeteries at Scarborough, Amersham and Tangmere:

Pilot Officer H W Moody, 30 years, Memorial panel No. 9.

Flying Officer W Coverley, 23 years, Dean Road Cemetery, Scarborough.

Sergeant M Sprague, 21 years, St Andrew churchyard, Tangmere.

Sergeant B Whall, 22 years, consecrated cemetery, Amersham.

Sergeant D Elcombe, 21 years, Memorial panel No. 14.

The first German aircraft to crash-land on British soil was this Heinkel HE 111, shot down by 602 pilots on October 28, 1939.

Battle of Britain – Phase 1

July 10 – August 7

The Battle of Britain was split into five phases, with the first beginning on July 10, 1940. At this time France was out of the war and the German forces were little more than 20 miles away from the English coastline. Britain was now isolated and had to turn her attention completely to the defence of the country. Anything that could possibly be turned into weapons was liable to be commandeered. The dangers were twofold: aerial bombing and the very real threat of an invasion.

The southern counties would be the frontline - the battlefield - and the defences in that area therefore had to be a priority. Barbed wire fences and mines were planted around the south coast. At the same time vast numbers of the civilian population were organised into the Volunteer Defence Force, later the Home Guard. They armed themselves with anything that could serve as a weapon, such as old guns, pitchforks and large pieces of wood which could serve as clubs.

Old cars and other vehicles were plucked from rubbish heaps and placed in fields and other open spaces as items of defence against enemy aircraft landing. Road signs were removed and obstructions were placed close to airfields, ready to be moved on to the landingstrip.

Fighter Command was desperate to build up the numbers of pilots at its disposal. Just before the Dunkirk debacle the average pilot strength of a squadron was 17 and by mid June their numbers had risen to 20, still a long way short of the target.

The workload of these pilots rapidly increased. They were told that they not only had to defend the country, repulsing the various

People's war: Spitfire funds boosted public morale by allowing ordinary people of contribute to the purchase of individual aircraft.

The Battle of Britain Clasp

In 1942 the Air Ministry decided to extract from the wartime records a list of all pilots who had lost their lives as a result of fighting during the Battle of Britain (August 8 - October 31, 1940) as a pre-requisite for the creation of a national memorial. These dates were later amended to include the period July 10 to August 7, so that the official dates accepted as the Battle of Britain were July 10 until October 31, 1940, inclusive.

During the period of the Battle of Britain, 2,917 men were awarded the Battle of Britain Clasp for having flown at least one authorised sortie with an eligible unit of RAF Fighter Command. These men came from the following countries:

Great Britain 2,334	Australia 33
Belgium 29	Canada 98
Czechoslovakia 88	France. 13
Ireland 10	Jamaica 1
Newfoundland 1	New Zealand 126
Poland 145	Rhodesia. 3
South Africa 25	United States 11

During the Battle of Britain 544 men lost their lives in the course of their duties. Between November 1, 1940 and August 15, 1945 a further 795 died in all theatres of war.

602 Squadron was one of the 14 Auxiliary Squadrons who took part in the Battle. These Auxiliary Squadrons were known as part time or week-end flyers, but whatever they were calledthey certainly made their mark – not only during the Battle of Britain but throughout the war.

On the seventh anniversary (July 10, 1947) King George VI unveiled the Battle of Britain Memorial in Westminster Abbey. It had been decided to dedicate the easternmost of the five small chapels forming the chevet of Henry VII's chapel to the memory of the men of the Royal Air Force killed in the Battle of Britain.

In September 1940 a fragment from a German bomb pierced the east wall of the chapel and the hole was retained covered with glass.

The centrepiece of the chapel was the memorial window extended to cover the entire east wall. The lower panes contain the badges of 63 squadrons that took part in the Battle, although in 1960 the number of units serving under Fighter Command during the battle was officially amended to 71.

enemy raids, but also would have to fly on special patrols over the occupied countries of France and Belgium.

Goring detailed two 'Fliegerkorps' containing a number of Dornier bombers, a Stuka unit and two fighter aircraft units. The two top Luftwaffe Aces, Major Adolf Galland (JG 26) and Major Werner Molders (JG 53), led these fighter units. They were a very strong battle group, numbering around 75 bombers, 60 Stuka fighter-bombers and about 200 fighter aircraft.

On July 2 instructions were issued for the campaign against Britain to begin. The following day small groups of bombers supported by fighters were out over the Channel searching for Allied shipping. British radar networks were unable to pick them up soon enough to give our fighters a chance to intercept.

On July 4 a flight from each RAF Sector Station was ordered to operate from its forward grounds. A few days later, Spitfires from 54 Squadron found themselves in bother when tackling a unit of Bf 110s near Dungeness. They were about to attack when they were themselves attacked by Bf 109s from a higher altitude. This resulted in two Spitfires being shot down and another damaged. One pilot was wounded.

One of the reasons why the Spitfires were caught out in this situation was the fact that the formations and tactics used were those from a bygone age *(See photograph p. 21)*. The lessons of Dunkirk had still not been digested. At this time the RAF squadrons were flying compact formations based on tight elements of three aircraft, and the tactics were standardised. There were five different forms of attack and it was the flight commander who decided the tactics to be used.

In modern aircraft these tactics were obsolete. After attacking the enemy bombers the planes would swing into line astern, and this manoeuvre offered their bellies to the bombers' gunners. The British soon followed the example of

This Spitfire, hit by return fire from a Junkers over Beachy Head, crash-landed in a field at Iford, near Lewes, on October 12, 1940.

their enemy and changed their formations and tactics, basing them on the German 'schwarme' of two pairs of aircraft: the British called it 'finger four'.

Each aircraft flew in a position corresponding to the fingers seen in plan view. In the formation, the leader was represented by the middle finger and the number two by the index finger, while numbers 3 and 4 took up the positions of the third and little finger. In this type of formation there is a better all round view which made it easier for each pilot to cover the others.

On July 10 Fighter Command found themselves fighting the opening phase of the Battle of Britain.

Equivalent Ranks

This list should assist the reader when comparing the ranks of the various airmen of the RAF and the Luftwaffe.

ROYAL AIR FORCE	LUFTWAFFE
Marshall of the Royal Air Force	Generalfeldmarschall
Air Chief Marshall	Generaloberst
Air Marshall	General
Air Vice-Marshal	Generalleutnant
Air Commodore	Generalmajor
Group Captain	Oberst
Wing Commander	Oberstleutnant
Squadron Leader	Major
Flight Lieutenant	Hauptmann (Hptm)
Flying Officer	Oberleutnant (Oblt
Pilot Officer	Leutnant (Lt)
Warrant Officer	Stabsfeldwebel
Flight Sergeant	Oberfeldwebel (Oberfw)
Sergeant	Feldwebel (Fw)
Corporal	Unteroffizier (Uffz)
Leading Aircraftman	Obergefreiter (Obgefr)
Aircraftman First Class	Gefreiter (Gefr)
Aircraftman Second Class	Flieger (Fl)

Stars of 602

*T*he idea of this chapter is to fill in some of the background as well as a few personal details of those brave pilots who defended the southern parts of England from their base at Westhampnett, Sussex, a satellite airfield of Tangmere - a number of whom have supplied me with autographed photographs. This is something of which I am fiercely proud.

Babbage, Cyril Frederick

Nicknamed 'Cabbage', he was born on June 25, 1917, at Ludlow, Shropshire.He was a quiet, shy sort of chap, tending to keep himself to himself, but a committed pilot who was involved in all the major combats throughout the Battle of Britain. He was almost always seen wearing his cravat.

He joined the RAF, becoming a sergeant pilot, and was a serving member of 602 in December 1939. He moved south with the squadron in August 1940. Between August 18 and 25, 1940, he shot down three enemy aircraft, with another shared, three of these aircraft being bombers.

A day later he was himself shot down over Selsey Bill by the Luftwaffe Ace Hptmn. Hans-Karl Mayer of 1/JG53, baling out into the sea. He was brought ashore at Bognor Regis, the subject of a famous photograph (*see p. 3*). He made several more claims during September and the early part of October.

On October 12 he attacked a Junkers Ju 88 in the Beachy Head area and was hit by return fire. He attempted to make his way back to Westhampnett but was forced to land at Iford, near Lewes. On landing, the aircraft tipped over.

Around this time he was awarded the DFM and a few weeks later was commissioned as a pilot officer. At the end of 1940 he was rested, and in June 1941 he was posted to

Members of 602 Squadron on the day war broke out. Seated left to right are Muspratt-Williams, Grant, Urie, Robinson, Boyd and Stone, with MacLean standing at front right.

41 Squadron. It was with this unit that, on September 18, he reported shooting down an enemy aircraft resembling a Curtis Hawk. In fact the aircraft was a Focker Wulf 190, possibly the first reported destroying of the new aircraft. The pilot of this plane was one of the great German Aces - Hptmn. Walter Adolph, a Knights Cross holder of II/JG26, who had at that stage a total of 25 Allied victories to his credit. Adolph's body was washed up on a Belgian beach about three weeks later.

Babbage later undertook a further tour of operations on Mosquitos, during which he was shot down twice. By the end of the war he had risen to the rank of wing commander. He remained in the RAF, instructing on A1 radar after the war ended, and subsequently became an admin. officer serving at RAF Stradishall in 1956. He retired in June 1964 and died in 1977.

Barthropp, Patrick Peter Colum

Known as 'Paddy', he was born in Dublin on November 9, 1920, during a visit to the city by his parents. He was educated at St. Augustine's Abbey School, Ramsgate, England by Benedictines and later at St. Joseph's College, Pell Wall Hall, near Market Drayton.

On leaving school he started work as an engineering apprentice with Rover Cars. In November 1938, aged 18, he obtained a short service commission. In September the following year he went to No.1 School of Army Co-operation at Old Sarum, and on his completion of the course he was posted to 613 (City of Manchester) Squadron at Odiham, where he flew Hinds, Hectors and Lysanders during the early part of the war.

On August 21, 1940, volunteers were called for to join Fighter Command and, after training, he joined 602 Squadron at Westhampnett. He was posted to 610 Squadron in December of that year and, after postings elsewhere, returned to Westhampnett in August, 1941 as a flight commander, being awarded the DFC the following month. He was rested in October and went to 61 OTU (Operational Training Unit) staying there until May 1942. He was posted out on May 12 to 122 Squadron, based at Hornchurch. On this occasion he drove to the base in his 'drop head' Rover car, a 21st birthday present some six months before. His flights were mainly sector reconnaissance and the odd convoy patrol. At this stage he had completed 317 operational flights with the loss of one Lysander and two badly holed Spitfires.

His war was shortly to end. Five days after arriving at Hornchurch he took off with a large number of aircraft including six Boston bombers to attack a factory near St. Omer, France. Flying at around 20,000 feet, the group was attacked by a number of Focker Wulfs from JG 26. It was at this time that he ignored advice that had been given to him by a very experienced pilot, Jim Hallowes. He was shot down by a FW 190 of JG 26 and baled out to become a prisoner of war.

Sent to the famous Stalag Luft III, he took part in the 'Great Escape' (made famous by the film). He was released in May 1945 and returned to the UK. In September he was sent to Norway to identify Allied air crew graves there. In January 1946 he attended the Empire Test Pilots' School at Cranfield and took command of 'A' Fighter Test Squadron for tropical tests, but on his return he was posted to HQ Fighter Command, as Ops Day. In March 1952 he became wing commander flying at Waterbeach for two years, for which he received an AFC in 1954. He left the RAF the following year.

Barthropp, who set up a successful high class limousine hire firm in Paddington with another war time fighter ace, Brian Kingcome, has written an amusing autobiography which shouldn't be missed. Very funny, he has been described as a 'barn-stormer', a 'raconteur', a 'chauffeur to the filthy rich', a 'bon viveur' and lots more.

He was once reprimanded for writing a confidential report on a junior officer, which read: 'Flying Officer Harvey is a scruffy genius. He thinks he is a genius, I think he is scruffy.' His one great complaint is that he has never been paid the money he is owed for his time as a POW.

He was credited with four destroyed (two shared), one probable and three damaged.

Boyd, Robert Findlay

Born in East Kilbride, Scotland on June 8, 1916. He worked as a mining engineer prior to the war, joining the Auxiliary Air Force in 1935, when he was posted to 602 Squadron. He was mobilised with the squadron in September 1939 and saw his first action over Scotland during the end of that year and the beginning of

Spitfires of 602 Squadron, B Flight, take off in their early outmoded Vic formation. (See p. 17)

1940. By the time the squadron was posted to Westhampnett he was a flight commander, and he enjoyed a great deal of success. He hated the Germans and vented his feelings on every occasion that he could. On September 24, 1940, he was awarded the DFC for nine victories. A Bar followed in October for three further victories. In December 1940 he was posted to 54 Squadron as commander, a position he held until July 1941. He was posted later that year to 58 OTU at Grangemouth, to 57 OTU (being promoted to wing commander) and to Tangmere (wing commander flying).

In February 1942 he was on a sortie with his station commander, Group Captain Victor Beamish when they spotted the famous German capital ships 'Scharnhorst' and 'Gneisenau' steaming up the English Channel. They quickly returned to raise the alarm.

He was awarded the DSO in April 1942 and then commanded Eglington airfield for a period in 1943. Later that year he was sent out to the Far East to AHQ, Bengal, from where he was posted to command 293 Wing on the Burma front at the beginning of April 1944. He made claims against Japanese aircraft while there, but no confirmation has been found. He was mentioned in despatches on January 1,1945.

AIR MINISTRY

Defining Enemy Aircraft

DESTROYED:
a. Aircraft must be seen on the ground or in the air destroyed by a member of the crew or formation, or confirmed from other sources, e.g. ships at sea, local authorities, etc.
b. Aircraft must be seen to descend with flames issuing. It is not sufficient if only smoke is seen.
c. Aircraft must be seen to break up in the air.

PROBABLES:
a. When the pilot of a single-engined aircraft is seen to bale out.
b. The aircraft must be seen to break off the combat in circumstances which lead our pilots to believe it will be a loss.

DAMAGED:
Aircraft must be seen to be considerably damaged as the result of an attack, e.g. undercarriage dropped, engine dropped, aircraft parts shot away or volume of smoke issuing.

He retired in 1945 as a group captain. After undertaking charter flights for Scottish Aviation, he tried his hand at pig farming and herring fishing and then ran the Ferry Inn at Uig, Isle of Skye. He died in 1975.

He was credited with 21 destroyed (seven shared) three probables and seven damaged.

Findlay Boyd stands on the right of this picture taken at the 602 home base of Drem in April, 1940, on the departure of Squadron Leader Farquhar.

Gillies, James

His home town was Intake, Yorkshire. He joined the RAF and was posted to 602 Squadron as a sergeant pilot in early September 1940. He was soon involved in the action, with a share in the destruction of a Junkers Ju 88 on the 21st and was credited with damaging two Bf 110s during the next few days -one of these being damaged while flying over Brighton on the 25th.

Early in October he was posted to 421 Flight, but on the 17th he crashed his Hurricane after combat with Bf 109s and was injured. In January 1941 the Flight became 91 Squadron based at Hawkinge, and in May he was awarded the DFM.

In November he was commissioned, and postings followed to 59 OTU; to 615 Squadron, accompanying the unit to India; to 22 Group; and to 136 Squadron, where he claimed two victories in May 1943 as a flying officer. His next posting was to 79 Squadron as a flight commander.

On February 13, 1944 he was awarded the MC by the Army for spotting and marking an ammunition dump for attack. During 1944 the squadron converted to Thunderbolts. However, on April 21, during the first operations flown from a new base at Myingyan North, he was shot down by A.A. fire in a Hurricane IIC HV546/2 and killed.

This is all that is known of a pilot who had been further promoted to flight lieutenant prior to his death. He is remembered on the Singapore Memorial.

He was credited with six enemy aircraft destroyed (one shared) two probable (one shared) and two shared damaged.

Hanbury, Osgood Villiers

Known as 'Pedro' because of his moustache. He was born in Richmond, Yorkshire, on September 13, 1917, and after completing his education at Eton went to Germany to learn the language. On his return he worked for Shell at Teddington and also joined the RAFVR in early 1939. He trained at 12 E&RFTS until March at Wick, before going to 13 E&RFTS at White Waltham, where he trained until August 1939. He was called up at the outbreak of war and received his commission in June 1940, becoming a Lysander pilot.

He transferred to Fighter Command just as the Battle of Britain began, being posted to 602 Squadron on September 4. He was involved in the thick of the action throughout the remainder of the year. Assessed as 'above average' at the end of his time with this unit, he was posted to 260 Squadron in May 1941 when it was just about to go to the Middle East. In December of that year he was promoted to flying officer.

The unit was equipped with Kittyhawks in 1942, and in April he was promoted to command, receiving a DFC a month later. A Bar was added in July. He was rested from July 19 until November 5, when he returned to command, leading the unit until the end of April 1943. He was awarded the DSO at this time. At the conclusion of the Tunisian campaign, he returned for a brief leave to the UK, where he got married.

'Pedro' Hanbury with his Spitfire at Westhampnett in the summer of 1940.

Hanbury perished on June 3, 1943, along with several other officers when their Hudson aircraft - returning to the UK - was intercepted and shot down over the Bay of Biscay by a Junkers Ju 88C of 15/KG 40 flown by Lt. Hans Olbrechte. Unbeknown to him, his new bride had become pregnant, and she gave birth to a son, Christopher, who was never to see his father. He was just 25 years old at the time.

He was credited with 12 destroyed (two shared), two probables and five damaged (two shared).

Johnstone, Alexander Vallance Riddell

Known as 'Sandy, he was born on June 2, 1916. Before the war he worked for Scottish Aviation Limited as an instructor at No. 1 Air Observation and Navigation School, and later at No. 1 Civil Air Navigation School, Prestwick.

He had joined 602 Squadron, Auxiliary Air Force, late in 1934 and was then mobilised with this unit in August 1939, becoming a flight commander early in 1940. On July12 he became commanding officer. He was involved in some early engagements around the Scottish coast. He shot down a Heinkel over Scotland during the night of June 26/27, flying a Spitfire. He was then involved in the shooting down of a Junkers Ju 88 on July 1 and damaging a Dornier Do 17 a couple of days later.

On August 13, 1940 he led his squadron south from Drem to Westhampnett , where they would be based throughout the Battle of Britain months. At the start of October he was awarded the DFC. He took his squadron back to Scotland on December 17.

About the middle of April 1941 he became controller at Turnhouse, but he

Just before the outbreak of war the RAF Auxiliary and Reserve forces were called up. This is Sandy Johnstone's 'call' to join No. 602 City of Glasgow Squadron, which he was to lead throughout the Battle of Britain.

was soon on the move once again, this time to the Middle East at HQ, 263 Wing, in Beirut. In April 1942 he found himself sector commander at Haifa, Palestine, before moving in September to Malta as the deputy commander at Luqa and then as controller.

The following January he returned to operations as wing leader at Krendi, but a couple of months later he returned to the UK to attend the RAF Staff

Sandy and Margaret Johnstone on their wedding day, January 27, 1940. He was to go on to a magnificent RAF career, leading 602 Squadron throughout the Battle of Britain.

College. He later held senior positions at Fairwood Common, Bentley Priory, General Eisenhower's HQ in France and the RAF delegation in Washington.

He remained in the RAF after the war, with postings to Dublin; the Air Ministry, Ballykelly in Northern Ireland; the Air Sea Warfare Development Unit at St. Mawgan; and Fighter Command at Newton. He was seconded to Malaysia at the time of Independence to help form the Royal Malaysian Air Force and, after returning to the UK in 1958, he first became station commander at Middleton St. George, then attended the Imperial Defence College before returning to the Air Ministry as Director of Personnel. In 1964 he was posted to Borneo as air commodore, Commonwealth Air Forces, during the Indonesian confrontation. He again returned to the UK in July 1965 to become an air vice marshall, and AOC 18 Group, doubling also as Air Officer Scotland.

Two NATO appointments followed, but at the end of 1968, he retired with a CB. Now in 'civvy street', he ran the National Car Parks operation in Scotland (also finding time to serve as secretary of the Glasgow Golf Club), and subsequently moved south to become an NCP director in London (as well as being secretary of Denham Golf Club). He was also the deputy chairman of the TAVR council for ten years.

Sandy Johnstone has written a number of books, chiefly based on a diary he kept during the Battle of Britain. He is currently living in Suffolk.

He was credited with nine aircraft destroyed (two shared), one probable, and six damaged (one shared)

Lyall, Archibald

Known as 'Pat', he was born in Glasgow in 1913, the son of a Highland Light Infantry officer who was killed in France in July, 1916. He enlisted in the Royal Air Force Volunteer Reserve early in 1937.

He joined the RAF, and was posted to 602 Squadron as a sergeant pilot on September 28, 1939, together with Andy McDowall. He received his commission as a pilot officer the following June.

Pat Lyall saw plenty of action during the Battle of Britain, being involved in all the major combats.

At 2.10 pm on Thursday November 28, while involved in combat over the Isle of Wight, he was shot down by a Bf 109. He baled out of his Spitfire too low and was killed. He was 27.

His mother requested that his funeral be held in the south of England so that as many of his colleagues as possible could attend. It was held on the afternoon of the December 8 at Brighton Crematorium.

He was credited with six enemy aircraft destroyed (three shared), two probables and nine damaged (four shared) - the latter including the damaging of a Bf 110 over Brighton on September 25, 1940.

Pat Lyall stands on the right in this photograph. He shot down six enemy aircraft, with a further two probables and nine damaged – one over Brighton.

On top of the world. Andy McDowall is the man in pole position in this picture of 'B' Flight, 602 Squadron.

McDowall, Andrew

Known as Andy, he was born in 1913 at KirKinner, Wigtownshire in Scotland. He worked as a Clydeside engineer, joining the Royal Air Force Volunteer reserve and being attached to 602 Squadron as a sergeant. He was mobilised at the outbreak of war in September 1939.

He became one of the most successful fighter pilots during the Battle of Britain. He was awarded the DFM on October 8, 1940, and a Bar was added two months later. Commissioned in late November,he stayed with the squadron until April 1941, when he was posted to 245 Squadron as a flight commander.

Some details of his later career seem to be missing, but it is believed that he became a service test pilot with Gloster Aircraft, testing the new Jet Meteor, because in July 1944 he took over command of 616 Squadron. This unit swapped its Spitfires for the first of these jet fighters.

He was promoted to wing commander and led the squadron until the end of April 1945, when he went with it to Holland to join 122 Wing.When he left the service he became one of Gloster's staff test pilots, later being awarded the AFC for this work. He died on the November 26, 1981.

He was credited with 13 enemy aircraft destroyed (two shared), two proba-bles and one destroyed on the ground – on April 24, 1945, in Germany.

McKellar, Archibald Ashmore

He was born on April 10, 1912, in Paisley, Scotland, but the family moved to Glasgow where his father started a plastering business. He attended Shawlands Academy for his education. He was a small man, just 5' 3" tall. *(See photograph page 8)*. He rather reluctantly joined his father's business, but he really wanted to fly – which in the main his father opposed. He took lessons secretly with the Scottish Flying Club at Abbotsinch, gaining his 'A' licence.

In 1936 he was invited to join 602 Squadron, being commissioned in November of that year. He was mobilised with them in August 1939 in the rank of flying officer. On October 28, 1939 he was involved in the destruction of a Heinkel He 111 which crashed in the Lammermuir Hills – the first German aircraft in the war to crash on British soil *(see page 9)*. He was promoted to flight lieutenant in June 1940 and posted to 605 Squadron as a flight commander. He was in action throughout the summer and autumn of 1940, his great success resulting in the award of a DFC on September 13. Later that month he took command of that unit as an acting squadron leader. He received a Bar to his DFC on October 8.

On November 1 his pilots lost sight of him during an engagement with Bf 109 fighter bombers over the Maidstone area. Eyewitnesses stated that his Hurricane was seen circling over Woodlands Manor, Addisham, apparently searching for a place to land. He had circled several times, when the aircraft suddenly flicked over on its back and crashed into the ground. It is thought that he may have been wounded and lapsed into unconsciousness. The first rescuers on the scene found Archie McKellar dead. It is probable that he was shot down by Hptmn. Helmut Lippert of II/JG27

The award of a DSO was gazetted on November 26, and a Mention in Despatches followed. His father visited Buckingham Palace to receive his decorations. On September 10, 1990 a commemorative plaque was unveiled at the crash site.

He was credited with 20 enemy aircraft destroyed (three shared), five probables and three damaged: surely one of the very best fighter pilots in the Battle of Britain.

Former Commanding Officer Sandy Johnstone was one of the signatories when the author was accepted as an associate member of the 602 Museum Association. It was formed, as the certificate explains, 'so that the history and traditions of the 602 (City of Glasgow) Squadron, Royal Auxiliary Air Force, are retained for all time as part of our nation's heritage'.

Battle of Britain – Phase 2

August 8 – 23

While the Luftwaffe Operations Staff anxiously awaited a good weather forecast for the opening of 'Adlerangriff', it was not as yet committed to an all out attack on the Royal Air Force fighter defence system.

For Fighter Command a new and serious phase of the battle began on August 8, when bombing was intensified. Fierce air battles developed, which resulted in higher losses on each side. A month of attrition began in which the RAF were strained to the absolute limit.

Goering was waiting for the weather to change so that he could annihilate the British air defences, a feat which he felt could be achieved in just a few days.

602 Spitfire at Dispersal, Westhampnett, 1940. Note the trolley jack on the left of the picture.

His intelligence officers had indicated to him that the RAF fighters would be no match for the vastly superior Luftwaffe. The numbers of aircraft had now been built up, ready for the attack.

The Reichsmarschall could not know that Air Chief Marshal Hugh Dowding was holding his forces in check, refusing to commit large numbers of fighters to a battle over the Channel where the warning time was short and the enemy had the advantage. Dowding took heart from a moderate but steady growth in personnel and, very soon, from a surprising but critical increase in aircraft.

Records show that on August 3 there were just 700 fighters available for operational work and about 1,400 pilots and air crew. This was a marked improvement on the figures some five or six weeks before, when there were 587 fighters and 1,200 pilots and air crew. On July 10 Fighter Command had 52 squadrons, and on August 8 these had been increased by three, with another six under training: these included No. 1 RCAF (Royal Canadian Air Force).

Most units in the groups rotated through satellite airfields for short periods, one of the exceptions being 602 Squadron, which remained in the front line for almost the whole length of the battle.

Flying Officer John Dundas, the older brother of Hugh 'Cocky' Dundas and a pilot with 609 Squadron, wrote in his diary: 'By the beginning of August, 609 were working to a settled operational programme with 238 and 152 Squadrons. 609 and 238 were based at Middle Wallop and 152 at Warmwell. The routine went as follows: a day on 15 minute availability at Wallop, a day of release off camp and a day of readiness at Warmwell, where we kept a servicing party of 30 airmen under Flight Sergeant Agar and Sergeant Fitzgerald.

'At this time Warmwell possessed, though in rather irregular proportions, the two chief characteristics of a forward station: Action and Discomfort. Every third day, at midday, the pilots were to set off from Wallop in squadron formation, their cockpits bulging optimistically with sponge bags, pyjamas and other articles of toilet which they got very little chance of using.

'Sleeping accommodation was provided for visiting squadrons in the sergeants' quarters, but after some experience of this, pilots preferred to accommodate themselves as best they could in the dispersal tent, which was, at least, furnished with beds, dirty blankets and an assortment of unreliable telephones.'

August 8

145 Squadron were based at Westhampnett immediately before the arrival of 602 squadron: it was 602 that relieved them. They were led by Squadron Leader John Peel and flew Hurricane fighters. On this day he reported: 'We climbed to 16,000 feet and, looking down, saw a large formation of Ju 87s approaching from the south with Me 109s stepped up behind at 20,000 feet. We approached unobserved out of the sun and went in to attack the rear Ju 87s before the enemy fighters could interfere. I gave a five second burst to one bomber and broke off to engage two

The officers' mess at Westhampnett, August 1940.

Me 109s. There was a dogfight. The enemy fighters, which were painted silver, were half rolling, diving and zooming in climbing turns. I fired two five-second bursts at one and saw it dive into the sea. Then I followed another up in a zoom and got him as he stalled.'

Going Down to Sussex

*I*t was just on midnight on the 11th August when Harry Moody and Pat Lyall burst into the crew-room. They were beaming with excitement and could hardly get their breath. They had been drinking down in the Royal Hotel at Drem and had heard some exciting news – or was this exciting news mere rumour?. The barmaid had casually mentioned that she'd heard the squadron were about to move to the south of England.

Surely that couldn't be true they told themselves. How could a barmaid possibly know? It was surely just a rumour.

Sandy Johnstone listened in astonishment, which soon turned to excitement and bewilderment. 'Down to the south' he repeated out loud. He couldn't contain himself any longer and quickly picked up the telephone to 13 Group HQ. Everyone was looking and listening, some with their mouths open, wanting to ask the question: 'Are we really moving south sir?' they wanted to know?

Sandy's face told them the answer even before he uttered a word, because a broad grin stole over his features. The voice on the other end of the line said 'Yes, that's right – the signal is on its way to you. You're off to Tangmere the day after tomorrow.'

Someone rushed across the room to look at the calendar, and shouted 'Yes; it's the 13th!' – a good or a bad omen?

602 ground crew at Westhampnett during the summer of 1940. Few pictures of ground crew appear in books, despite their importance. [602 Squadron museum]

Hardly anyone got any sleep that night, so intense was the excitement.

The morning of the 13th dawned and everyone was up early, their small bundles of belongings packed. The main luggage and the ground staff and other personnel would travel down separately.

The sixteen Spitfires sat gleaming, the Merlin engines snarling, exhausts popping, the pilots sitting in the cockpits waiting for the signal from Johnstone. Padre Sutherland was there, saying his last farewells together with the station commander.

A wave of the hand from Sandy and they were off, rolling across the grass, faster, their speed picking up. Soon they were airborne, the sun glinting from their wings. They made one circuit of the air base, dipped their wings and set a course southwards – off for the biggest adventure in their history.

They made a beautiful sight as they became smaller and smaller in the summery sky. Then the Spitfires quickly turned into small dots and were gone.

Two 'kills' for this Spitfire pictured at Westhampnett in September, 1940. [602 Squadron museum]

Baptism of Fire

*T*uesday August 13, 1940 was a famous date in the calendar of the
Luftwaffe. The German High Command named it 'Adler Tag' (Eagle
Day). On this day the German air Force flew a total of 1,485 sorties - the
launch of a campaign to beat the Royal Air Force into total submission so that
England might be invaded by the German military who were just across the
Channel and almost ready to move. They were gathering together a vast armada
of boats of all types and descriptions. There is no doubt that the invasion would
have been very real if the Royal Air Force had been beaten.

With this in mind it was decided that 602 Squadron would be moved south
from their Scottish base at Drem to the small airfield at Westhampnett in West
Sussex. When the order came through, one pilot was heard to remark: 'Where
the hell is that? It ain't even on the map!'

Westhampnett was
a new satellite of
Tangmere, an airfield
that many of the pilots
of the day had, indeed,
heard of.

Sandy Johnstone
later recalled: 'I awoke
early to the sound of
heavy rain battering
on the window and,
looking outside, was
presented with a bleak
scene of muddy
puddles and dark rain

*'At readiness'. A Spitfire of 602 at the Westhampnett
base. Within days of the squadron arriving, it had to
repel a vicious German attack on Tangmere.*

clouds. It was hardly an auspicious start to our great adventure.'

The sixteen Spitfires (twelve front line aircraft plus four reserves) were soon
lined up and ready to go. The ground crew had already loaded the Harrows
with the equipment that had to be transferred to their new home, and they set
off at ten o'clock. As noon approached, the Spitfires were lined up in flights of
four, with Sandy Johnstone in the lead flight. They were seen off by the
commanding officer and Padre Sutherland, complete with bagpipes. They were
soon airborne and climbing steadily, breaking clear of the cloud at 15,000 feet
and then turning southwards: their adventure was just beginning.

Eventually landing at Westhampnett, they taxied across to one end of the
field and the pilots - slowly getting out of their machines - found it hard to
believe what they saw. Near the centre of the field was a Hurricane on its back

while, glancing over towards one of the boundary hedges, they could see a pall of dark smoke rising into the air.

The Harrow aircraft had already arrived, and the ground crews were already unpacking the equipment. Westhampnett was very basic: three fields had been knocked together to make it into an airfield. The pilots had a thatched cottage as their billet. The ground crew, not so lucky, had a building which had been used as dog kennels, the smell still lingering.

Pilot Officer Glen 'Nuts' Niven, who was just 20 years old, later summed up their new home: 'It was just a field. We were on our own - no bloody officers bumbling about. A farmhouse was our mess and about half the pilots (me included) lived in a nearby thatched cottage with no furniture except mattresses on the floor. Your suitcase acted as a chest of drawers. On the field itself were a couple of Nissen huts where we were to spend our days on "Readiness" '

Johnny Peel, 145's commanding officer, welcomed Sandy Johnstone with his arm in a sling. 'It's been pretty rough,' he said. 'We could do with a bit of a rest.'

There squadron had just five Hurricanes left. Four were serviceable and the fifth was in the field upside down. 145 couldn't wait to leave, and as soon as the formalities had been completed - which took about two hours - they were off. It was a straight swap: their new base was to be Drem, the airfield from which 602 had just left. The Hurricanes were quickly airborne, wasting no time in taking a northerly direction.

Two of the 602 pilots, Paul Webb and Hector Maclean, strolled across the grass to examine their new home, starting off with Woodcote House. There wasn't much to see, apart from the Nissen huts. There was a grubby, tattered windsock dangling from its post, its limpness reflecting the general feeling of a number of the pilots.

The current senior controller at Tangmere was David Lloyd, who had flown with 602 Squadron a few years previously. The commanding officer was Group Captain Jack Boret. He arrived at Westhampnett a couple of hours after the arrival of 602, bringing glad tidings to the new encumbents of the airfield.

'It's been a bit rough,' he told Sandy Johnstone. ' You'll probably have to make five or six sorties a day, as well as some night flying two or three times a week.'

That sort of news did nothing to lift the gloom the pilots were feeling at this time. The following day they were sent up on seven separate occasions, without any real significant incidents to report.

The first real wartime incidents occurred two days later on August 16. It was rather a warm day with just a hint of sea haze. Several pilots were stretched out on the grass enjoying the sunshine. Among this group were Dunlop Urie, Findlay Boyd and Hector Maclean. It didn't appear to them at this moment that there was a war on. They were engaged in a little bit of light-hearted banter among themselves. It was approaching lunch time when Sandy Johnstone joined them.

'Anyone for a beer?' he asked

Mickey Mount, relaxing in a chair nearby, replied in a lazy manner: 'Yes, I'll have one. What's for lunch? '

They were in the officers' mess tucking into spam, vegetables and boiled potatoes when the nearby telephone uttered its shrill call.

'Get airborne quickly!' ordered the Tangmere Controller. 'There are twenty-plus approaching from the south.'

The telephone was quickly replaced, with the shout: 'Villa Squadron scramble', then with added zest: ' Scramble, at the double!'

One of the pilots glanced at his watch. It was just coming up to 1pm. The pilots were on the run, hurtling across to their Spitfires. The ground crew had donned their tin hats and were already getting the powerful Merlin engines bursting into life as the pilots began to arrive. There was an air of excitement: this was it, the real thing. Other members were helping the pilots adjust their straps - everything was being attended to at the double. Just seconds later and, almost as one, the aircraft began to roll forward ready for takeoff. Gradually picking up speed, off they went, one after another.

In quieter times. This photograph was taken at Drem in April, 1940, when the ferocity of the August dog-fights could hardly be imagined. Back row (left to right): f/p Coverly, f/o Webb, f/o Jack, w/o McIntosh, f/o Grant, f/o McKellar, f/o Ferguson and f/o Ritchie. Front row: f/o Urie, f/l Robinson, s/ldr Farquhar, f/l Johnstone, f/l Boyd.

'That was great,' said one of the ground staff as they watched them climbing into the sunny skies. 'Just like the pictures.'

It was at about the time they became airborne that the sirens from nearby Tangmere could be clearly heard.

As the Spitfires climbed the R/T's were filled with Sandy's urgent voice: 'Villa Squadron, Villa Squadron, orbit base at Angels 2.' 'A' Flight, commanded by Dunlop Urie, made it to the pre-arranged meeting point but the others were already sweeping across the West Sussex countryside. The fight was on.

As the squadron had lifted from their base, they had seen the waves of German aircraft coming in, flying in perfect formation. These were recognised as Junkers Ju 87B Stuka dive bombers. The Stukas were soon over Tangmere and were beginning their dive, the scream from their engines sounding out well above the racing Merlin engines as they struggled to hit top speed. The Bofor guns then added to the noise.

Almost at once, the bombs from the dive bombers started to explode on Tangmere. One scored a direct hit on a hanger, blowing it apart, pieces lifting high into the air. Next to go was a stores building, which was completely demolished - smashed to matchwood. Another hanger, narrowly missed by a bomb, was badly damaged by the blast. Yet another bomb made a large crater very close to the runway. Blast damage was also responsible for the cracked walls at the control centre: the building was now windowless and glass was spread over a wide area.

Several Hurricanes were badly damaged as the bombs rained down. Over the radio came David Lloyd's voice: 'Come on chaps, get the blighters, get them!' The Hurricanes of Tangmere 43 and 601 Squadrons were by now also involved and attacking the Stukas, while the Spitfires of 602 were engaged with the Bf 109s and 110s, the accompanying escort aircraft. The sky was filled with cannon fire, aircraft were twisting and turning, as first one then another would try for the kill. It was a desperate confrontation.

During the struggle a voice was heard on the R/T: 'They've got me. The plane's been hit - returning to base.'

It was Glyn Ritchie, who dropped from the skies, keeping an eye in case he was attacked by one of the enemy. He made it safely back to base unhurt, and his aircraft was able to be repaired.

Meanwhile, high above, the R/T was filled with different voices as dozens of different scenarios were played out. The Spitfires and Hurricanes were certainly excelling themselves as one after another German aircraft headed downwards.

It was tempting to watch a bomber going down, waiting to see the huge splash in the sea, but that was a dangerous thing to do. The dogfight needed all of a pilot's concentration, as aircraft were flying in all directions. One was heard to say: 'Christ, I've got one, he's going down. Look he's in the water!' Another exclaimed:'I've got two.' Then a succession of voices: 'Look out Blue 3, behind you- brake, brake!' . . . 'Green section, go for those bombers, go for the bombers: Tally ho!' . . . 'Bandit, 10 o'clock!'

A Hurricane was seen on fire, trailing smoke as it headed down towards the sea. Almost at the same time an ME110s canopy was blown apart, the aircraft flipping over and going almost straight down. Pilot Officer Harry Moody, attacked one of the Stukas as he came across in front of him, but before he could take any action he was hit himself: 'I've copped one - returning to base.'

As he approached, the aircraft caught fire, but he landed it safely. Unhurt, he was nevertheless a little wiser for his experience. The aircraft, was later able to be repaired.

Meanwhile, the action continued, a Spitfire chasing a bomber, another Spitfire and a Hurricane dealing with a pair of Stukas.

At about this time a Hurricane of 601 Squadron was attacking a Junkers Ju 87 over Bognor. Both pilots fired at each other simultaneously and both aircraft were hit. The Junkers hurtled almost vertically straight downwards and crashed into the sea. The Hurricane, streaming glycol with a hint of fire, made its way back to Tangmere. The pilot, Bill Fiske, struggled with the controls, his aircraft now well alight, but managed to crash-land the machine. He was pulled from the cockpit and rushed to hospital, very badly burned. He died the next day - probably the first American pilot to die in the Battle of Britain.

Findlay Boyd, ('B' Flight's commander) had barely become airborne, his undercarriage only partly up, when a Junkers Ju87 Stuka appeared over the trees, having just released its bombs on Tangmere. He corrected his aim, and the first burst put the German dive-bomber into the ground: they could never have seen him.

The Spitfire banked round, completing just one circuit, put the wheels down and landed. Boyd went over to the crashed Ju87, helped himself to a luger pistol and a Leica camera, the crew becoming prisoners. He had been airborne for less than a minute - surely, the quickest kill of the war.

A smiling face for the camera filming A Yank in the RAF in 1941, the aircraft scenes for which were flown by 602 Squadron. Bill Fiske, a 601 Squadron Hurricane pilot killed in action this day, is believed to have been the first American pilot to die in the Battle of Britain. He is buried in the churchyard at Tangmere.

As the skies at last cleared, Sandy's voice came over the R/T system: 'Home boys. It's all over.'

Gradually, the Spitfires returned to base, the pilots exhilarated by their success. One by one they made their way across to report to Henry Grazebrook, the squadron's intelligence officer, who was seated at a small table close to the 'A' Flight dispersal area. The combat reports were eagerly filled in, the claims

being checked and rechecked. The picture of the battle was gradually becoming more clear. The enemy had come across the Channel in strength and had then separated. Their targets had been not only Tangmere but the RDF station at Ventnor, the naval station at Gosport and the airfield at Lee-On-Solent.

It emerged that Sandy Johnstone, Dunlop Urie and Paul Webb had managed to get among the escorts and hit at least six of them. Then, of course, there was

Findlay Boyd's Stuka, while Nigel Rose and Andy McDowall had attacked the Junkers Ju 87's, one of which crashed down into the sea, with two others officially classed as 'probables'.

Even as this was happening, the Spitfires now at dispersal were being re-armed and refuelled, ready for the next sortie, whenever that might be.

During this attack, 43 Squadron lost four Hurricanes on the ground, all being classed as write-offs. In the air, they lost another four aircraft and one pilot killed, with another pilot suffering a minor injury.

By the end of the combat, the German losses included two Me 110s shot down, another trailing smoke as it crossed the Channel. There was also at least one damaged as the battle ended. Three Bf 109s were shot down and another two were involved in a mid-air collision, with one of the pilots killed. The Junkers Ju 87s

Tangmere ablaze. The hangars are smashed and burning after the Stuka attack at midday on August 16, 1940. This was 602 Squadron's 'blooding' in the Battle of Britain.

41

fared a lot worse, with eight shot down, the crews of seven of them being killed. There were another seven Junkers Ju 87s damaged, some having to crash- land near to their home bases.

Over at Tangmere, the clouds of black smoke, which could be seen for miles, indicated the huge cost to the airfield. The station commander, Group Captain Jack Boret, looked around and shook his head in disbelief at the chaos caused in such a short time. One of the hangers that had been hit contained four very valuable aircraft - all lost. Yet another hanger was on fire. The station work-shops, a pump house and an air raid shelter had received direct hits. The officers' mess and a Salvation Army hut were severely damaged.

Some of the ancillary buildings had also been hit, their contents strewn across the roadways. The station was an absolute mess, with furniture, fittings and reams of paper almost covering the lawns in front of the HQ building. The water and electricity mains had been severed. One of the worst hit buildings was the sick bay, almost totally demolished. A number of personnel had been wounded, some seriously, and were being treated.The sick and injured were lying everywhere.

Broken aircraft were all around, some minus wings, others in dozens of pieces. A couple more had been hit by flying debris. To one side, was a Hurricane, still on fire, the aircraft of Bill Fiske, who was slowly losing his fight for life at the station sick quarters.

The final total of aircraft damaged or destroyed were one Magister, six Blenheims and seven Hurricanes. As well as the aircraft, it was noted that almost 40 motor vehicles of various types were either destroyed or badly damaged.

Doc. Willey, 602's Medical Officer, was hailed a hero, performing a number of miracles, rescuing trapped personnel and treating a number of victims with ghastly injuries in this horrific attack. He carried out his life-saving work in various places all around the station. He was still working tirelessly throughout the afternoon and well into the evening. For his outstanding performance on this day he was awarded the Military Cross.

Sandy Johnstone arrived and reported the efforts of 602 Squadron to Jack Boret who, still shocked, replied simply: 'Good show Johnstone, good show!'

'The Hardest Day'
August 18

Sunday August 18, another bright and sunny day, was destined to become known as 'The Hardest Day' - and for the pilots and ground crews of 602 it was certainly going to be one that would never be forgotten.

The morning started rather quietly and leisurely by wartime standards, with some pilots busying themselves with writing letters to friends and loved ones while others read or played chess. A group of German POW's had been sent to Tangmere to help clear up the mess that their comrades had made a couple of days earlier.

It was a strange life at this time: one minute you were 20,000 feet up, fighting for your life, and the next you were sitting in the sun, enjoying an English country garden. The enemy had given no cause for combat for the past 24 hours and this was a time to enjoy the lull, not knowing just how long it would last.

Lunch-time arrived and the officers' mess was noisy with general chat and some 'micky-taking' over in the far corner, the laughter carefree and boisterous.

The C.O., Sandy Johnstone, had been on night patrol over the Isle of Wight and had been diverted to shoot down a loose barrage balloon. Although he had emptied all his ammunition into it, it

Part of an ammunition belt taken from the rear gun of a Stuka forced down on August 18 by Basil Whall. One of Whall's rounds smashed through the cartridge on the right without detonating it.

continued flabbily on its way and was last seen drifting over Portsmouth. He handed the responsibility of the squadron to Dunlop Urie.

At just after 1pm the alarm sounded. The pilots weren't dressed for flying, but grabbed their parachutes and flying helmets as they ran. Urie reached his

Spitfire first and *(see below)* was astounded to find it jacked up with its wheels off: the ground crew had been working on it. Nearby, however, was a brand new machine, which had been delivered just a couple of hours earlier - there hadn't even been time to paint the squadron letters LO on it. He climbed in.

Tangmere, meanwhile, was scrambling 601 and 43 Squadrons, while help was requested from 10 Group: the Spitfires of 152 and 234 squadrons took off

Dunlop Urie recalls The Hardest Day – and the most short-lived Spitfire of them all!

(This story is written on four small sheets of paper which are now in my collection)

"We had been at Westhampnett about a week and had been on 'readiness' most of the time, from 05.30hrs to 21.00hrs each day - ready to get the squadron into the air at five minutes notice. On August 18 we at last got a long awaited 'release' which meant we were not liable for duty, except at two hours notice.

His injured feet bandaged, Dunlop Urie waits to be taken to hospital.

We went over to the lovely house which was our mess and sat down to lunch with a pint of beer at our side. I had taken two swallows of this when the phone went. Could we take off as soon as possible? All the Tangmere squadrons were engaged and there was a raid which seemed to be coming for Tangmere again.

We ran the quarter of a mile back to our aircraft. I had been leading the squadron before we were released and automatically assumed I would still be leading. When I got to my aircraft I found its wheels were off. A new aircraft had been delivered that morning. I grabbed my parachute from my own aircraft and ran for the new one. Its guns had not been tuned up with the sights, but it seemed important to get airborne to lead the squadron. I reckon we were airborne from the mess in about five minutes.

We were up and ordered to patrol Tangmere at 2,000 feet. I think they were still feeling the raid on the 16th. Someone spotted Ju 87s dive bombing Ford, a naval aerodrome about five miles east of Tangmere, and with a 'Tally Ho' we made for them. There were two wings each of about 24 aircraft. As I dived down after the second wing, Findlay Boyd, who was leading 'B' flight, called up on R/T that he would look after the fighters. I must say, I was so incensed with the Ju 87s that I hadn't seen the Me 109s. The Ju 87 had always seemed to from Warmwell and the Hurricanes of 213 squadron were called in from Exeter. Their target was the largest formation of German aircraft to attack this part of the southern coast throughout the whole of the war. It was a staggering sight.

The leader of this enemy armada was 32 year old Major Helmut Bode in a Junkers Ju87 of the 3rd Gruppe of Geschwader 77. Their base was at Caen in France, but they had been assembled in forward positions around Cherbourg.

me the meanest aircraft the German's had. They used it as long range artillery to terrorise fleeing civilians in Belgium and France.

I decided that shooting them down didn't matter so much as sending them back badly damaged and wounded. I reached the formation just as it was pulling up having dropped its bombs. I went right through it and fired at the aircraft before I ran out of ammunition. As I was pulling away, having shot at them, the controller called me up to ask if I was engaged. There was a machine on my tail and I didn't look at it carefully enough in my mirror. As I was

thinking how to reply to the Controller, I thought it was another Spitfire. However, as I started to answer on the R/T I was disillusioned. There were four loud bangs and I was blasted out of my seat by an Me 109.

I didn't dare take violent evasive action - anyway I couldn't until I regained my seat. He had another go and hit me several times again and then pulled off. I thought of baling out but was too low, so I collected myself and returned to Westhampnett. My R/T

Spitfire X4110 had a service life of just 27 minutes. It was delivered to 602 Squadron on the morning of Sunday August 18, 1940. Flown by Dunlop Urie, it was severely damaged in action over Bognor Regis and never flew again.

was destroyed and I had no flaps and, it transpired, no brakes - and both wheels punctured. I came in over the trees to Westhampnett and my guardian angel was watching over me. We made a good landing and I waited for the ambulance.

My legs and parachute were full of shrapnel. Fortunately the fuse of the Me 109s cannon shells had been set a fraction too soon and the shells exploded on impact with the skin of the Spitfire. Hector MacLean, who succeeded me in command of 'A' Flight, had a similar experience about a fortnight later. The fuse was more delayed and a shell exploded in his leg. *"*

Bode had been briefed to attack the radio station at Poling, near Littlehampton. He was leading more than a hundred Junkers Ju 87s Stuka dive bombers, their bombs prominent for all to see, flying in perfect formation.

A few hundred yards behind Bode's gruppe came Hauptmann Alfons Orthofer's 2nd Gruppe, their target being Ford Naval Air Station. A few hundred yards behind them, and a little to the left, was the 1st Gruppe, led by Hauptmann Herbert Meisel, who was bound for the Coastal Command airfield at Thorney Island. Last came the 1st. Gruppe of Dive Bomber Geschwader 3 led by Hauptmann Walter Siegel, their target the naval air station at Gosport. Each one of the Stukas carried a 550 pound bomb under the fuselage and four 110 pounders under the wings.

The German escort aircraft didn't take off until their dive bombers were well across the Channel, because the Stukas were travelling at only 120 miles per hour and the fighters with their superior speed could easily catch them up before they crossed the English coast.

As the formations approached the coast, the radar station at Poling reported them first as '80 plus' approaching, then as the minutes ticked away there were further sightings on the screen: '20 plus', '12 plus', '10 plus' and so on - these smaller numbers being the escorting fighters as they caught up with the Stuka bombers. Helmut Bode, glancing around, felt very confident as he surveyed the escorts now getting into position. This wouldn't be difficult, he thought.

The advantage the Spitfires and Hurricanes had was that they had been given sufficient warning and were already airborne and waiting. Even so, they didn't expect to see such huge numbers of enemy aircraft approaching. And so the stage was set . . .

Poling was the first target to be struck as Bode led his dive bombers in, their bombs falling in great abundance. The station was already getting a pasting, the bombers having a field day. The buildings below the 350ft mast were being obliterated: the damage was massive.

602 Squadron were heading for the formation attacking Ford (2nd Gruppe) and very soon they were sighted. Dunlop Urie, the leader, radioed Tangmere: 'Villa Squadron, bandits over Ford, tally ho.' By this time the whole squadron were itching to get among the Stukas. Urie directed Findlay Boyd to attack the Bf 109s, the escort fighters, while he led 'A' flight into the attack against the Stukas, who in turn were in their dive prior to releasing their bombs.

Meanwhile, down below, the station staff were searching for shelter against this massive attack. They witnessed their station being ripped apart. One of the fuel tanks received a direct hit and exploded, sending sheets of flames skywards. Some buildings were already a pile of rubble as walls collapsed inwards, their roofs shattered and ripped open. Hangers suffered very heavy damage , with collapsed walls and heavy doors being blown off. Seventeen aircraft were destroyed on the ground, a number hit by large pieces of debris.

Wounded and dying people lay everywhere, writhing in pain, some suffering terrible injuries. Indeed, this surprise raid resulted in one of the most serious death tolls from a Luftwaffe attack on any airfield throughout the war: the final total was to be 28 personnel killed and 75 wounded.

Urie, totally hyped up, went in for the kill, firing at everything that bore the German colours. He hit four of the Stukas before he used up all his ammunition. One of these Stukas appeared to stop still in mid-air for a long time before it slowly turned over and hurtled earthwards, its crew still on board. Another of Urie's four simply swung away to starboard and went straight down : no parachutes were seen to come from it. Urie pulled away, glancing momentarily to either side, and was aware of an aircraft close behind him. At this point he thought it was his No. 2, but then it fired from both wings: it was a Bf 109, one of the escort aircraft.

He said later: 'I thought my world had come to an end. The cockpit filled with a tremendous noise, a crashing, ripping and rendering sound. I lost control, the stick pulling out of my hands. I fell

German Bf 109 fighter plane such as this escorted the huge formation of bombers which attacked Tangmere and its surrounding bases on August 18, 1940.

forward, as if someone had given me a violent push in the back. I was aware of searing pains in my legs.' There was a brief pause and the aircraft was hit again, this time in the tail section.

'I now really reckoned that I was a goner,' Urie recalled. 'I thought one more time and I was dead.'

Luckily, the Bf 109 pilot thought that he had done enough damage to the Spitfire and left it to crash, heading out to sea, hightailing it for home after the rest of the German aircraft .

Somehow, Dunlop Urie made it back to base, landing minus flaps and with a burst tyre, his Spitfire badly damaged. He was helped out of his plane, having been shot in the lower part of both legs. It was later found that his parachute pack had been so badly damaged as to have been unserviceable. His aircraft had had a service life of just 27 minutes. He was taken to hospital at Chichester with his legs full of shrapnel.

While this episode was unfolding, Ginger Whall had been eyeing up his opponent, a Junkers Ju 87 of the second formation. He gradually gained on it. Engines screaming, the two planes flew low over the streets of Bognor, Whall drawing closer and closer, his finger poised. 'Not yet, not yet,' he told himself. 'I must make sure.' He was now little more than fifty yards behind. He fired four measured bursts from his guns just as the Junkers Ju 87 turned, striking it along the fuselage. Whall saw small pieces of the fuselage chip off and fall away. He was getting ready to give the German plane a final burst when he saw the aircraft start to bank into a gentle curve. This was now like slow motion compared with the speed over the Bognor streets just a short time before. He watched it continue to bank, the curve getting slowly wider as if it had all the time in the world and wasn't really part of the battle at all.

He continued to watch as the curve deepened. Turning northwards, the plane re-crossed the coastline with Whall still waiting to give it another burst - but there was no need. The German dive bomber gently descended, its skilled pilot in complete control as it dropped lower and lower. The aircraft, although badly damaged, made a near perfect landing along the fairway of the 16th hole at the Ham Manor Golf Course, near Poling. The pilot was captured, but his fellow crewman had been killed.

As the aircraft landed, Whall opened the throttle and climbed away heading seawards after the fleeing aircraft. Incredibly, he caught up with one of the Junker Ju 87's which had delivered its bombs and was now making its way home. He attacked it from an acute angle from about fifty yards and emptied the remainder of his ammunition. His aim was true: the bullets struck the cockpit and the engine area, and the aircraft immediately burst into flames, its fuel tanks holed. The Stuka keeled over and headed straight for the sea.

Whall saw a trail of smoke behind him and suddenly realised that his Spitfire had been hit. He didn't want to go down into the sea but, glancing at his

In the rough. Members of the local Home Guard protect the Junkers Ju87 forced to land at Ham Manor Golf Course after being attacked by Ginger Whall.

controls, he discovered that the oil pressure showed zero and the temperature was rising. He gently eased the aircraft around, coaxing her: 'Come on girl, get me home.' He felt pretty pleased with himself, although a mite lucky, as he touched down at Elmer Sands at Middleton. Switching off and climbing out, he breathed a sigh of relief. Looking skywards he could still see the aircraft above him, twisting and turning. The battle wasn't over yet - although it was for him.

High above the ground, 'B' Flight were engaged with the Bf 109s of JG 27 and JG 53. The six Spitfires making up this flight were outnumbered by something like eight or nine to one. The skills of these young pilots were certainly being put to the test today. They kept their turns really tight, easily out-manoeuvring the Messerschmitts. They were picking their targets with great gusto, and one by one those targets were going down.

It was essential at a time like this that they watched each others' backs as much as possible, their contact being via the R/T system. It would be quiet for only seconds at a time, and then a voice might shout: 'Villa Leader, Villa Leader, 10 more at 12 o'clock', followed by someone else hollering 'Blue 3, lookout, break, break' and another voice hissing 'Jesus, he just missed me'. Then would come the unmistakable voice of Findlay Boyd: 'From Villa Leader - come on, let's get 'em!'

Leading them in, Boyd picked out a diving Bf 109 which was frantically trying to escape. Boyd, his finger poised on the firing button, was just waiting for the right moment. His guns fired a short burst and the Bf 109 went straight down. Boyd saw that he was now over Ford airfield, black smoke still rising. He singled out a Stuka dive bomber: another short burst, another hit. He left that one and made off after another Stuka. Again his guns spat fire and another aircraft was on its way down. He saw a Stuka crash down into the sea off Selsey Bill. No parachutes were seen from these aircraft, and the crews were therefore presumed to have been killed.

Andy McDowell was involved in a one-to-one with a Bf 109. In a tight circle they went, getting ever tighter. The Bf 109 was no match for the Spitfire under these circumstances.

'A little more, come on, come on,' McDowall muttered, his finger poised on the button. His patience was soon rewarded. He saw his bullets strike the fuselage and cockpit, the pilot slumped forward, and in those few seconds it was all over, the aircraft heading down towards the sea.

Despite these kills, however, the 602 boys weren't having it all their own way. On a number of occasions the Messerschmitts broke through, trying to protect their bombers as well as to destroy the Spitfires. Ian Ferguson had hit two Stuka bombers during his combats, and as he attacked and shot at his third he felt his aircraft give a shudder. His aircraft had been hit by 20mm cannon shells in three places - the port wing, the elevator and fuel tank. It was soon showing a vapour trail, the plane becoming very difficult to control. He had to make a quick decisionwhether or not to bale out. Within a few seconds he was over Littlehampton. He could see the streets and could just about make out people below him. The idea of baling out was quickly forgotten as he battled with the controls.

He was now flying pretty low but at a speed a little too fast for landing. He selected a grassy field just north of Littlehampton and was coming in just about

right, but what he didn't notice were the high tension cables that suddenly appeared immediately in front of him. They carried 33,000 volts and it was impossible to avoid them. The Spitfire propeller slashed through four of the six cables and Fergson was temporally blinded by a massive flash. He had lifted his hand in an effort to shield his eyes as he hit them. The Spitfire was thrown violently sideways before it crash-landed in the field at Norway Farm, Rustington.

It was about 2.45pm. Locals who had seen the aircraft come down rushed to the scene. By the time they had got across the field Ian Ferguson was out of the cockpit. He was found half-standing and half-leaning against his aircraft, cursing and swearing so incomprehensibly that, initially, the rescuers thought that he was a foreign pilot: Polish they guessed.

Flying Officer Ian Ferguson. His Spitfire sheared through electric cables before crash-landing at Rustington.

In fact Ferguson wasn't usually the swearing and cursing type, but the experiences of the past few minutes had been somewhat provoking. He was soon on his way to hospital to be treated for back injuries.

The next member of the squadron to get hit was Mickey Mount. He was just lining up on a Stuka when he was hit by a Bf 109 over Ford airfield. Both of his wings were shot through, his hydraulic system put out of action. He felt the aircraft hit, but now he had the problem of his controls being stiff and almost inoperable as he battled with his aircraft.

He decided that he would try to get back to base or, if necessary, drop down at Tangmere. Although he had problems with the controls, he managed to reach Westhampnett where, with luck on his side, he made a satisfactory landing. His plane would never fly again.

Harry Moody was feeling quite pleased with himself as he saw the Stuka bomber he had just attacked roll over and go crashing down. The smile that spread across his face quickly vanished, however, as he was attacked by four Bf 190s, one of these being no more than sixty

Mickey Mount. He fought with the controls to land his stricken plane at Tangmere.

yards away from the rear of his Spitfire. His aircraft shuddered as it was hit, waiting at any moment to be hit again. He dived down as fast as he could in a desperate attempt to shake them off, heading for the airfield at Ford Naval Station. The German pilots must have thought it certain that he was going to crash because, with a quick nonchalant glance, the four Bf 109s headed off across the Channel for home.

Pilot Officer Harry Moody.

Moody, extremely relieved, pulled out of his dive close enough to Ford to see the utter chaos at the airfield. Many of the buildings were on fire, others just a heap of rubble. People were rushing about in the mayhem, rescuing and caring for the wounded. Changing his mind, he headed for Tangmere. The Spitfire had had one of its tyres shot through and, although he landed it safely, it ended up on its nose. This aircraft, too, would never fly again.

As if by magic, the skies now quickly cleared, the Germans having turned back across the Channel. One by one the Spitfires made their way back to Westhampnett. Hector Maclean and Cyril Babbage had both hit Stukas, and as they left their machines they were soon swapping tales, their gesturing hands demonstrating the various combats.

Without any doubt, the luckiest pilot of the day had been Dunlop Urie. An eye witness stated that he 'came in screaming low over the trees, the holes in the aircraft making the noise. The wheels touched down, then bounced, the aircraft bounced again, the brakes had gone and so the Spitfire carried on across the field. The ambulance was already on the move. Further and further the Spitfire went, but it was now beginning to slow down, slower and slower, and then at last, stopped. The ground crew were already running to the scene of the stricken aircraft. The ambulance was the first to arrive.'

On his arrival at the hospital Urie was allocated a bed next to an ex-colleague from his days at Drem, Flight Lieutenant Nicholson. He was now the commander of 72 Squadron, and later in the war he would be awarded the VC for his deeds - the only one awarded to a RAF officer throughout the war. (As for Dunlop Urie, more than twenty years after The Hardest Day an eye specialist detected a shrapnel splinter behind one of his eyes. As it wasn't inter-fering with his sight it was decided to leave well alone. It is still in place today.)

At the de-briefing it was announced that five Stukas had been destroyed during the battle, with two others badly damaged and two Bf 109s shot down. Other squadrons had accounted for another ten Stukas, with a number of others damaged. Another six Bf 109s had also been shot down or damaged. The scale of the victory can be judged by the fact that, as a result of the combat on this day, the German High Command decided that the Junkers Ju 87 (Stuka bomber) would never come to England again in strength.

The British pilots, however, suffered their losses. A number of Spitfires and Hurricanes had been shot down, and all of the squadrons taking part lost some of their aircraft: apart from the two Spitfires lost by 602 Squadron, 43 Squadron had a Hurricane shot down, the pilot, Fl/Lt Carey being wounded; 152 Squadron had two Spitfires badly damaged, although they returned to their base with the pilots unhurt; and 601 Squadron had two Hurricanes shot down, their pilots lost, while another Hurricane crash-landed at Tangmere, the pilot unhurt.

More Stars of 602

Aries, Ellis Walter

Ellis Aries joined the RAFVR as an airman, trainee pilot in July, 1938 and was called up for service on September 1 the following year. He completed his training in June 1940, converting to Hurricanes at 5 OTU, Aston Down and joined 263 Squadron, a unit reforming at Drem after losing most of its pilots when the aircraft carrier HMS Glorious was lost after returning from Norway.

On July 5, 1940 he was posted to 602 Squadron. On the 26th he claimed a Dornier Do 17 destroyed off Selsey Bill. He claimed another Dornier shot down near Biggin Hill on September 7. In the same battle his Spitfire was damaged by return fire and he had to make a crash-landing at Wrotham, Kent.

He was 'grounded' and, to use his own words, put in charge of a room full of registered mail at Tangmere. He eventually returned to flying and later became an instructor. On January 1, 1945 he was awarded the AFC. By the time the war ended he was at the Empire Central Flying School. He was released from the RAF in 1945 as a flight lieutenant. He died in 1976.

Coverley, William Hugh

Hugh Coverley was commissioned in the RAFO in December 1936 and called to full time service at the outbreak of war. In June 1940 he was serving with 602 Squadron at Drem, and on July 7 he shared the destroying of a Junkers Ju 88. He moved with the squadron to Westhampnett in August, 1940.

He was shot down by enemy fighters over Dorchester on August 25, baling out unhurt. He was shot down again on September 7 over the Biggin Hill area and, unobserved, baled out badly burned. He landed in a tree, and his body was not found until September 16. His Spitfire crashed in flames at Fosters Farm, Haysden Lane, near Tonbridge. He was 23 years old and was buried in Dean Road cemetery, Scarborough. (*See page 79.*)

Eade, Arthur William

Eade was educated at Midhurst Grammar School, Sussex and joined the RAF as an aircraft apprentice in January 1929. In December 1931 he passed out as an aircraft fitter on aero engines. He trained first as an observer and then as a pilot, joining 602 Squadron at Westhampnett on August 13, 1940.

A further posting the following December took him to 610 Squadron, and on March 19 the following year he was involved in a 'sweep' just off Calais and was shot down by a Bf 109, sustaining shrapnel wounds in his shoulder and arm. He managed to return across the Channel and made a forced landing near Hailsham. After several other postings, he was awarded the AFC on June 2, 1943. He was released from the RAF in September 1947 as a warrant officer.

Edy, Allen Laird

'Jake' Edy's home was in Winnipeg, Canada, and after coming to England he joined the RAF on a short service commission in November 1938. He responded

to the call for more fighter pilots in August 1940 and went to 7OTU at Hawarden to convert to Spitfires, joining 602 Squadron on September 8, 1940.

He claimed a Dornier Do 17 destroyed on the 15th and on November 5 was awarded the DFC. Edy was shot down by Bf 109s on December 12 near Folkestone, crash-landing uninjured at Shorncliffe, Kent.

He was later posted first to 315 (Polish) Squadron and then to 457 (RAAF) Squadron. On December 12, 1941 his aircraft caught fire. He baled out but was too low, the parachute failed to open and he was killed. He was 25 years old. He is buried in St. Andrews churchyard, Andreas, Isle of Man.

Elcome, Douglas William

He was a native of Leigh-on-sea, Essex and joined the RAFVR in 1937 as an airman-trainee pilot. He was called up on September 1, 1939. He completed his flying training at 14 FTS, Cranfield in early June 1940 and, after converting to Spitfires, joined 602 Squadron.

On August 31 he destroyed a Bf 109 over Dungeness. On September 10 he crashed on the golf course at Felpham during night flying practice and wrecked his Spitfire. On October 26, at the age of 21, he failed to return from a routine patrol. He is remembered on the Runnymede Memorial, panel 14.

Fisher, Gerald

Gerald Fisher joined the RAF on a short service commission in November 1938. He did his initial training at 13 E&RFTS, White Waltham, and moved on to 7 FTS, Peterborough on January 31, 1939. In August 1940 he was at 7OTU, Hawarden and joined 602 Squadron at Westhampnett on September 8.

He claimed a Bf 109 destroyed on October 29. He was released from the RAF in 1946 as a squadron leader. He died in 1973.

Gage, Douglas Hugh

He worked as an architect before joining the RAFVR as an airman, trainee pilot. He was called up in September 1939 and, after completing his flying training at 7 OTU, Hawarden was commissioned and posted to 616 Squadron at Coltishall.

On September 21 he was posted to 602 Squadron at Westhampnett. Six days later he was jumped by a Bf 109 and made a forced landing at Bivelham Forge Farm, Mayfield. On October 30 he was involved in a surprise attack by Bf 109s over Dungeness. His aircraft was damaged and again he was forced to make a crash-landing, this time in Kent. He was again uninjured.

On June 6, 1941, aged 23 years, he was killed while serving with 91 Squadron at Hawkinge. He is remembered on the Runnymede Memorial, panel 32.

Hart, John Stewart

John Hart hailed from Sackville, New Brunswick, Canada, was at Mount Allison University and learned to fly at the Halifax Flying Club. In January 1939 he joined the RAF on a short service commission. He converted to Spitfires and, after first joining 54 Squadron at Catterick, he moved to 602 Squadron at Westhampnett.

On October 29, 1940 he claimed a Bf 109 destroyed, and on November 13 he shared a Junkers Ju 88. In early 1941 he was with 91 Squadron, but he went back to 602 for a while and then moved to OTU as an instructor. He commanded 67 Squadron in Burma from May to July 1943, and 112 Squadron in Italy from April to August 1945.

He was awarded the DFC on 22nd June 1945 and released from the RAF in 1946, his rank then being squadron leader.

Hopkin, William Pelham

Known as 'John Willie', he became a great friend of 'Nuts' Niven. Born in March 1921, the son of a parson, he joined the RAF on a short service commission at the tender age of 18. With his training completed, he converted to Hurricanes and

joined 54 Squadron at Catterick. On August 15 he damaged a Junkers Ju 87; three days later he claimed a Dornier Do 17 destroyed, a Bf 110 shared and another damaged; and on August 22 he claimed a Bf 110 destroyed.

On September 12 he was posted to 602 Squadron and his tally of German aircraft continued. On the 26th he claimed Heinkel He 111, the following day a Bf 110 and on November 6 a Bf 109 as a probable. Landing on November 23, he misjudged his height and came in on top of his C.O.'s parked Spitfire, writing off both aircraft. He was promoted to flight commander in early 1941. On May 24 he and Sergeant Brown collided on take-off: Brown was killed, but Hopkin managed to land safely back at base.

At the end of his operational tour, on September 9,1941, he was awarded the DFC. He stayed with the RAF after the war, serving in the secretarial branch and eventually retiring in 1967 as a wing commander. He was the first hon. secretary of the Battle of Britain Association when it was formed after the war. After two years' study he followed his father into the church, becoming a vicar in the See of Salisbury, but two years later he died of a heart attack.

Jack, Donald MacFarlane

Donald Jack was born on May 5, 1914 at Brookfield in Renfrewshire. He joined 602 Squadron, AuxAF in 1936, aged 22 years and was called up for service on September 4, 1939.

While the squadron was based at Drem he damaged a Junkers Ju 88. He moved with 602 to Westhampnett in August, 1940. On August 25 he claimed a Bf 110 destroyed, and on the following day a Bf 109.

In May 1941 he was posted to RAF Turnhouse to form and command 123 Squadron, which flew convoy and shipping patrols in the Firth of Forth area and trained pilots from OTU before they were posted to other squadrons in the south. In April 1942, the squadron went to the Middle East and, having no aircraft, was attached first to ADU and then to 274 Squadron in the Western Desert. When 123 Squadron was split, part of it merged with 80 Squadron and Donald Jack took command of 80 Squadron at El Bassa, Palestine, on September 17, 1942. The squadron moved to the Western Desert on October 12, and he was posted to Air HQ, Air Defence Eastern Mediterranean, Cairo, in February 1943.

He was promoted to squadron leader flying 243 Wing to take part in proposed landings on Rhodes, and was appointed SASO at HQ 209 Group at Haifa. He later took command of HQ 12 Sector at Port Said, returning to the UK in March 1945 and becoming station commander at RAF High Ercall two months later.

He was released in September 1945 as a wing commander, but he rejoined 602 Squadron in September, 1946 as adjutant and served with them until March, 1948. He is currently living in Scotland.

MacLean, Charles Hector

Hector MacLean joined 602 Squadron AuxAF, in 1936 and was called to full time service on August 24, 1939. On December 22 he shared the destruction of a Heinkel He 111 which was laying mines some 15 miles east of the Isle of May. On July 7, 1940 he shared in the destruction of a Junkers Ju 88.

He went to Westhampnett with the squadron, and on August 26 (*see pages 72–3*) he was shot down, crash-landing at Tangmere. Seriously wounded, he later had part of his leg amputated and thereafter took part in no more operational flying.

He left the RAF in 1945 with the rank of wing commander, becoming a senior partner in a well-known firm of Glasgow solicitors. His leg continued to give him trouble after the war and he had to undergo further surgery. He currently lives in Scotland.

Moody, Henry Woollaston

Henry Moody (*pictured on page 49*) joined the RAFVR as an airman trainee/pilot in 1937 and was called up on September 1, 1939. After completing his training, he joined 602 Squadron at Drem in March, 1940 as a sergeant pilot. Later that month he slipped while climbing into his Spitfire, fell and broke his collar-bone. He was commissioned three months later, on June 6.

He travelled to Westhampnett with the squadron in August, 1940. On August 16 he claimed a Bf 110 destroyed in the Brighton area ,and two days later claimed a Junkers Ju 87 destroyed. The following day it was *his* turn: while attacking a Junkers Ju 88 over Bognor, his Spitfire was set on fire, and he baled out with badly burned hands. He landed just outside Arundel, his aircraft crashing at North Bersted, north of Bognor.

On September 4 he claimed a Dornier Do 17 destroyed. While engaged in combat over the Biggin Hill area on September 7, he failed to return to base and was reported as missing. He was 30 years of age and is remembered on the Runnymede Memorial, Panel 9.

Niven, Hugh Glen

Nicknamed 'Nuts' (*see pages 115-118*) he was born in Toronto, Canada, on
September 23, 1919, but left six months later, and at the age of 18 years we find
him in Scotland. He joined 602 Squadron, AuxAF at Abbotsinch on May 7. 1937
and began his flying training with Avro Tutors. He was called to full time
service at the outbreak of war, converting to Hurricanes at 5 OTU at Aston
Down.

On September 1, 1940 he joined 602 Squadron at Westhampnett but, having
no Spitfire experience, he was posted to 601 Squadron on Hurricanes. Three
days later, however - after much complaining - he was posted back to 602 ,
where he quickly learned the art of flying Spitfires.

On October 29 his aircraft suffered damage during combat with a number of
Bf 109s over Maidstone. In late July 1941 he served a few days with 603
Squadron but was soon back with 602, where he stayed until September 23 - his
21st birthday. He was confined to sick bay for a couple of days and was then
admitted to Horton Emergency Hospital at Epsom, Surrey suffering from tuber-
culosis. He was invalided out onMarch 12, 1942 as a flying officer. When 602
Squadron was reformed in June 1946, he rejoined as a civilian clerk.

Payne, Roy Ainsley

Roy Payne joined Class 'F' of the RAF Reserve before the war as an airman,
trainee pilot. Like many others, he was called up for service on September 1,
1939. He volunteered for Fighter Command in August 1940 when the call went
out for more fighter pilots. On the 23rd he was posted to 7OTU at Hawarden.
He completed his course on converting to Spitfires and then joined 602
Squadron at Westhampnett on September 3, 1940. He was promoted to flying
officer on June 7, 1941 and fight lieutenant exactly a year later.

There appear to be no other details or records about him until his name
appears on RAF lists dated January 1944. There is no trace of his being wounded
or becoming a prisoner of war.

Proctor, Jack

Jack Proctor was born in 1917 and hailed from Coventry.
In April 1937 he joined the RAFVR as an airman trainee
pilot. He was called up on September 1, 1939, and after
completing his training he joined 602 Squadron on June
21, 1940 at Drem, travelling south with the squadron in
August to Westhampnett.

On August 31 he claimed a Junkers Ju 88 destroyed,
with a Bf 109 destroyed on September 6 and two Bf
110's destroyed on September 7 and 11.

He was killed on April 18, 1941, aged 24 years. He is
buried in St. Michael's churchyard, Stoke, Coventry.

Ritchie, Thomas Glyn Findlayson

Thomas Ritchie came from Dumbartonshire and joined the RAFVR in 1937 as an airman trainee pilot. He was commissioned in March, 1939. Called to full-time service at the outbreak of war, he joined 602 Squadron at Abbotsinch in September 1939, moving to Westhampnett in August, 1940.

On August 19 he shared the destroying of a Junkers Ju 88, his first 'blood.' Four days later he returned to base with his Spitfire slightly damaged after being in collision with an unidentified British fighter in cloud. He was unhurt.

On August 25 he claimed a Bf 110 which he shot down over the Channel during combat in the Dorchester area. On the early afternoon of Friday September 6, during heavy combat with Bf 109s over Hailsham, he suffered serious wounds to his legs. He managed to get his damaged Spitfire back to Westhampnett and was then admitted to Chichester hospital.

In March 1941, now a flying officer, he was put in command of 'A' Flight. On the morning of July 21 the squadron escorted three Stirling bombers sent to attack a target near Lille, France. On their way they were 'jumped' by Bf 109s and he was shot down west of Lille and killed by Obfw. Marz of the 2nd Gruppe, JG 26. He was Marz's 4th victim. He is buried in Reninghelst church-yard extension, Belgium.

Rose, Stuart Nigel

Stuart Rose was born on the 18th June 1918 and was a trainee surveyor when he joined the RAFVR at Southampton in March 1939 as an airman trainee pilot. He began his pilot training at 3 E&RFTS, Hamble and had logged 87 hours before being called up at the out break of war.

After spells at No. 1, ITW, Cambridge, 14 FTS, Kinloss and 14 FTS, Cranfield (where he completed his training), he was posted to 602 Squadron at Drem, moving to Westhampnett with the squadron in August, 1940.

On August 25 he claimed a Bf 110 destroyed followed by a share in the destruction of another Bf110 on September 7. Two days later he suffered injuries which kept him out of the air for about a month. On October 29 he made another 'destroyed' claim against a Bf 110.

On June 18, 1941 he was promoted to flying officer and he was later posted to 54 Squadron at Hornchurch. Several other postings followed during the course of the war, including two spells in the Middle East at BGS, El Ballah.

He was released from the RAF in February 1946, as a squadron leader, and qualified as a chartered quantity surveyor in June 1948.

Smith, William Bruce,

Bill Smith joined the RAFVR in September 1938 as an airman trainee pilot. He was called up for full time service on September 1, 1939. He completed his training and was posted to 602 Squadron at Westhampnett on October 6, 1940.

On October 29 he claimed a Bf 109 destroyed, but the following afternoon he was shot down and wounded after being surprised by an attack by Bf 109s in the Dungeness area. His Spitfire crash-landed on the foreshore at Greetstone, near Lydd in Kent.

He did not fly again, being classed as medically unfit. He died on June 17, 1975.

Sprague, Mervyn Herbert

Mervyn Sprague was born on May 27, 1910 at Richmond, Surrey, was educated

at St. Paul's School and then worked for his father's chartered accountancy firm. He joined the RAF class 'F' reserve in 1935 and the RAFVR three years later, doing his weekend flying at No. 1 E&RFTS, Hatfield. He was called to full time service in September 1939, and in October was posted to 4 EFTS at Brough. He had postings at No. 3 ITW, Hastings, 4 FTS at Kinloss and Cranfield before joining 602 Squadron at Drem on June 18, 1940, moving to Westhampnett in August.

He was shot down on August 25, crashing into the sea off Portland: he baled out unhurt and was rescued. On the afternoon of September 11 he was shot down off Selsey Bill and killed. His body was washed ashore at Brighton on October. 19. He is buried in St. Andrew's churchyard, Tangmere, West Sussex.

Urie, John Dunlop

Dunlop Urie joined 602 Squadron, AuxAF in June 1935 and was called to full time service on August 25, 1939.

He shared in the destruction of a mine-laying Heinkel He 111 fifteen miles east of the Isle of May Isle on December 22. In April 1940 he was appointed flight commander. He damaged a Junkers Ju 88 on July 9, some ten miles east of Fifeness. On August 1 he tore the wing off his Spitfire, but emerged unhurt, while trying to land at Drem in awful weather conditions.

He travelled south with the squadron in August 1940. On August 18 he landed back at Westhampnett minus his aircraft's flaps and with a burst tyre, his Spitfire severely damaged by Bf 109s over Ford. He suffered serious shrapnel wounds to his legs and was taken to hospital. (*See pages 42-3.*)

On November 13 he shared in the destruction of a Junkers Ju 88, and the following month was posted to 52 OTU at Aston Down. He later commanded

151 Wing in Russia. He was released from the RAF in 1945 as a wing commander and became not only a partner in a firm of solicitors in Scotland, but a leading light in Clyde yachting circles. He is currently living in Australia.

Webb, Paul Clifford

Paul Webb was born on March 10, 1918 and was educated at Kelvinside Academy in Glasgow. He joined 602 Squadron AuxAF in1937 and was called to full time service on August 24, 1939 while working for the National Bank of Scotland.

On October 6 he shared in the destruction of a Junkers Ju 88 over the Firth of Forth. On July 1, 1940 he damaged a Junkers Ju 88 which then dropped its bombs harmlessly over the sea off Dunbar before crashing at Melun-Villaroche, France. A week later he damaged another enemy aircraft, a Heinkel He 111, but there are no further details of the fate of this aircraft.

On August 16, 1940, he shared in the destruction of a Bf 110, and on the 25th he destroyed two others. The following day he shared in the destruction of a Heinkel He 59. On September 4 he damaged a Bf 110, and three days later he shared another Bf 110. On this day, during combat with Bf 109s over Mayfield, East Sussex, his Spitfire was damaged and he made a crash-landing in woods near Boxgrove. He suffered injuries which included a broken wrist.

In early 1941 he was posted to 58 OTU, Grangemouth as an instructor, and he later went to 123 Squadron at Drem, as a flight commander. In November of that year he took command of 416 (RCAF) Squadron, which was then forming at Peterhead. On December 1, 1941 he was promoted to squadron leader. He led this squadron until March 1942, when he received a posting to the Middle East.

His next assignment was to command 253 Squadron in Italy from May to September 1944, when he was promoted and posted to command a wing. On October 17 he was awarded the DFC , and he later served in Yugoslavia.

After the war finished he commanded 612 Squadron and later spent four years as air attaché in Turkey. On January 1, 1963 he was awarded the CBE. He retired from the RAF on March 18, 1973, aged 55 years, as a group captain, retaining the rank of air commodore.

He is currently living in Wales.

Whall, Basil Ewart Patrick

'Ginger' Whall joined the RAFVR around July, 1937 at the age of 19 years, and was called to full time service at the outbreak of war. He attended the 11 Group Pool at St. Athan. Around this time he was flying Gladiators and was posted to

605 Squadron at Tangmere on September 20, 1939. In April the following year he was posted to 263 Squadron and on the 21st embarked on HMS Furious bound for Norway. Three days later he landed his aircraft on a frozen lake in Norway. By nightfall on the 26th all the Gladiators were either unserviceable or had been destroyed. The following month a second expedition was made to Norway, and on May 21 the squadron began patrolling. He destroyed a Dornier Do 17 on the 23rd and destroyed two further enemy aircraft before the squadron was withdrawn on June 6. On September 24, 1940 he was awarded the DFM for his services in Norway.

On July 5, 1940 Whall was posted to 602 .On August 16 he shared in the destruction of a Dornier Do 17, and two days later he destroyed two Junkers Ju 87s. During the combat with the Junkers Ju 87's, his Spitfire was damaged by return fire and he crash landed at Elmer Sands, Middleton. On August 26 he claimed two Heinkel He 111's destroyed, followed by a Bf 109 on the 7th, a Dornier Do 17 on the 9th and a Junkers Ju 88 shared on the 30th.

On October 7 (*see pages 112-13*) his Spitfire went out of control in mysterious circumstances after a successful attack on a Dornier bomber in the Brighton area, crashing near Court Farm, Lullington. He was taken to the Princess Alice Hospital at Eastbourne with serious injuries and died on admission.

He is buried at St. Mary's churchyard, Amersham, Buckinghamshire.

Whipps, George Albert

George Whipps joined the RAFVR in December 1937 as an airman trainee pilot. Called up for service in September, 1939, he was posted to 602 Squadron at Drem on completing his training the following June.

At about 1.30pm on September 6, 1940 he was shot down in combat over Hailsham. He baled out unhurt, his aircraft crashing at Pelsham Farm,

Peasmarsh. On October 29 he claimed a Bf 109 destroyed.

In August 1941 he was posted to 61 OTU, Heston as a flight sergeant instructor. On the 26th he was with a pupil in Master No. W 8583 when a Belgian pilot in a Spitfire failed to check the runway before taking off and sheared the hood off the aircraft, killing both occupants immediately. The Belgian pilot was killed himself on November 6 when a Spitfire landed on top of his taxying aircraft.

George Whipps is buried in St. Mary's churchyard, Theydon Bois, Essex.

Battle of Britain – Phase 3

August 24 – September 6

For four days, between August 19 and 23, the weather was extremely cloudy and overcast, and this gave some respite to the combatants of the opposing air forces. The German senior commanders called a meeting at Karinhall for discussions regarding their fighter escort problems. It appeared to them that Fighter Command was holding back on some of its squadrons, despite the alleged heavy losses. It was essential to the German High Command that all aspects of the RAF be involved in the battle, because supremacy in the air was of vital importance before the invasion of Britain could begin.

*A posed picture of a squadron intelligence officer, or 'spy',
debriefing pilots after combat. In reality the pilots would
have taken their helmets off first.*

The Luftwaffe had itself received heavy losses: 127 medium bombers and 40 Stuka dive-bombers in the two weeks to August 23. The heavy loss of the Stuka dive-bombers was significant as it resulted in their being withdrawn from the battle to be kept in readiness for the invasion.

On August 20 a directive from Goering was issued which gave the order for airfields and aircraft factories, rather than the Channel convoys, to be the main targets. It was decided that a great many Bf 109 escort fighters would be needed, and so the fighter strength of Luftlotte 3 was moved to airfields closer to the Channel, many being deployed in the Calais area.

At this time Fighter Command was taking stock of its own position, believing that an invasion could be imminent. In the second phase (between August 8 and 18) no fewer than 94 pilots had been killed or posted as missing, while another 60 had been wounded in varying degrees. In this disastrous situation a great and urgent effort was made to recruit more pilots.

There had been a slight improvement around the beginning of the month, but as the days passed these numbers had been eroded. The pilots of the front line squadrons were exhausted by the long hours of fighting and the constant wear on their nerves.

There was, however, to be better news regarding the aircraft situation. The losses had been horrific during the second phase of the battle: 54 Spitfires,and 121 Hurricanes totally destroyed; 40 Spitfires and 25 Hurricanes damaged beyond unit repair; and another 30 aircraft destroyed on the ground, making a total of 270 aircraft in less than two weeks.

The production of replacement aircraft was now stepped up, with the aircraft factories working around the clock. The repair depots were working flat out, and in some cases damaged aircraft were repaired and back on station within 24 hours.

August 25

S unday August 25, 1940 started somewhat dismally, appearing full of rain, but as the morning wore on the clouds began to break and the sky slowly lightened.

The Battle of Britain was now entering its third and crucial period. Airfields all over southern England were under continual attack, and serious damage was being inflicted. Most of the German Bf 109s were being transferred to the airfields around Calais in order that they should have the shortest possible flight across the Channel.

During this morning the squadron, on standby, was scrambled twice to deal with reported German aircraft out over the Channel, but the enemy proved to be elusive and no contact was made. The Luftwaffe seemed to be teasing - trying to draw the English fighters out. Lunch, for once, was taken at a leisurely pace, with plenty of time to relax afterwards.

At about 5pm, with a chill in the air, the radar screens showed up a very large formation building up off the western part of France, close to St. Malo. Its direction was taking it over Cherbourg and then towards the Channel Isles. There was intense discussion between those watching the screens as to what the target might be. As the minutes passed, tracking the intruders became a little easier: they appeared to be making for the Weymouth area.

The operation telephone rang,there were a few hurried words from the young pilot who answered it and Sandy Johnstone and a dozen of his men were soon sprinting across to the waiting and readied Spitfires. They hurriedly settled into their cockpits, the ground crews assisting with the final prepara-tions, and then within seconds the wheels were turning and, one by one, they were away - off to work!

Johnstone, in the lead, took them up in close formation, flying westwards. They reached a height of 15,000 feet and levelled off: they needed the advantage of the height against the incoming German aircraft.

Findlay Boyd, ever watchful, was the first to spot them: 'Villa Leader, Villa Leader, bandits 11 o'clock. Fighters above and behind.' Johnstone's decision was instant: 'Villa Squadron, tally ho! Blue leader, the fighters; Red and Yellow with me.'

This was the moment when the stomach rolled with anticipation, the heart came up into the throat and the eyes widened as the Spitfires went down with gathering speed, combat about to begin.

Boyd took his group in a wide sweep, their engines racing. The remainder of the Spitfires went straight for the bomber formations of Junkers Ju 88s and Heinkel He 111s, which scattered immediately the Spitfires were spotted.

The six Spitfires made very good passing shots on them, hitting several, but before the pilots could assess the damage, the escorting German fighters were among them. It then became a whirlpool of mixed aircraft. Around and around they went, the hunters indistinguishable from the hunted. The Spitfires of 602 had been joined by the Hurricanes of 17 Squadron from Tangmere. The fighters from 10 Group were also coming in to assist - 87 Squadron from Exeter and 152, 213 and 609 Squadrons from Warmwell.

The air waves were crazily busy: 'Jesus Christ, look at that!'; 'I've got one'; 'That blighter's on his way down.' A Messerschmitt 109 went crashing into the sea, quickly followed by a second. Yet another, crash-landed at Buckland, the wounded pilot becoming a prisoner. A Messerschmitt 110, trailing black smoke, hurtled earthwards, the crew baling out, both wounded: two more POWs. Another crashed and exploded, their crew killed. Two Junkers Ju 88s, badly damaged, just made it back across the Channel before they crash-landed, their crews wounded. Another Junkers Ju 88 crashed into the Channel with no survivors. The allied fighters were having a field day, although not entirely escaping, as two of their Spitfires and several Hurricanes were shot down.

Sandy Johnstone recalled later: 'I had dived below the melée to take stock of the position and had just started to climb again when a burst of tracer whizzed past my port wing tip. I had a quick flashback of Harry Broadhurst warning us that if we saw tracer being used it was odds on it was being fired as a sighter, so, praying he was right, I immediately side-slipped towards it, whereupon another tell tale streak passed up my starboard side.

'A quick glance in my mirror showed a Bf 109 glued to my tail. I pulled hard back on the stick, expecting it to pass underneath. He was a wily character and clung on. I continued to urge every last ounce of power out of the trusty Merlin, but it was too much for it, and I suddenly flicked over in a violent stall turn. The manoeuvre must have taken Jerry by surprise, for he hesitated momentarily, and before he could get out of the way I was almost on top of him. He presented a broadside target - one which even I couldn't miss. I can still see the look of agonised surprise on the German's face when his canopy shattered around him and the Messerschmitt went down in an uncontrollable spin, from which it never recovered. I followed him down until he crashed into a spinney on the outskirts of Dorchester and burst into flames.'

Meanwhile the battle continued.The time was now around 5.45pm. Some of the bombers dropped their loads and scampered back across the Channel, but the battle was still raging. A Messerschmitt Me 110 had Mervyn Sprague's Spitfire in his sights, Sprague could take no avoiding action as the formidable double 20mm cannons opened up. Within seconds the Spitfire was trailing smoke. As it rolled away to port he tried to correct it, but he realised that it was impossible.The sea looked none too inviting, but there was no choice: he managed to release the cockpit hood and bale out, his parachute billowing. He was soon struggling in the sea, just off Portland Bill, to be pulled out unhurt by a Walrus amphibian rescue aircraft.

The Spitfires were having a lot of trouble getting at the bombers because the ME 110s and escort ME 10's were making an excellent job of protecting them.

Donald Jack, professional as ever, was desperately trying to getthrough - and perhaps trying a little too hard. He suddenly found himself engaging with five German fighters at once. He used all his skill to dodge them and found himself turning in a very tight circle, so tight that he found himself surrounded by German ME 110s. Now it was a desperate case of survival. He shot at one, which quickly broke from the circle, and in a flash he aimed for this gap and was out and away: probably one of the most dangerous moments of his war.

Meanwhile, Findlay Boyd was really fired up and earning his reputation of becoming a professional killer: he hated these Germans. He had changed the range of his guns, reducing it considerably. He took any chance or even half-chance to get at the German aircraft. He attacked an ME 109E just west of Weymouth, hitting it fair and square, his bullets taking out the engine. It keeled over to starboard and went straight down into the sea, taking its pilot with it. He gave a momentary glance at it, but there were more still to get. He eyed up another, taking aim: a short burst of his deadly guns and it was heading the same way as the first - downwards.

Roger Coverley and Paul Webb were also in the thick of it. Having both just missed being hit, they ended the battle unscathed, but both claimed to have damaged a German aircraft last seen trailing black smoke over the Channel. Coverley was anxious to get a 'kill', and soon the opportunity presented itself. He took careful aim at an ME 110 and watched as the bullets struck home right along the fuselage. He waited a split second for it to go down, but it didn't. He was about to have another go at it, when he felt an unmistakable judder to the

'A' Flight's dispersal hut at Westhampnett, 1940.

rear of his plane. He knew he had been hit, but at that stage he didn't know just how badly. An ME 109 had got him from behind and now - crash! - he hit him again.

This time the fuselage was struck. The engine burst into flames, covering the cockpit and making it impossible for the pilot to see out. The aircraft stalled for a moment, leaned over to port, again stalled and then dipped nose first. Coverley mercifully managed to guide the Spitfire into a slipstream, and in that split second he was able to get out, very relieved when his parachute opened and he drifted down to make a safe landing. The Spitfire meanwhile, with trailing smoke and flames, continued its death dive. It crashed at Galton Heath, close to the A352 between Dorchester and the Warmwell airfield.

Paul Webb, high above the main action and watching his chance, selected his target and, with engine screaming, dived down with all guns blazing. His aim was true, and he watched with satisfaction as the German aircraft fell away. The crew, probably mortally wounded, never left the crashing aircraft.

Cyril Babbage was one of the few who did manage to penetrate the escort cover and get through to the bombers. He had already damaged one of the escort aircraft, and now he found himself in an almost perfect position to attack the ME 110 that presented itself before him. His first burst struck the very tip of the starboard wing tip. He edged a little more to port and let fly. This time no mistake - the aircraft fell away just as two parachutes opened and swung down to earth. He was now through to the bombers, and with finger poised on the firing button he made for one of the Dornier Do 17s which loomed large almost immediately in front of him. Having worked hard to get himself into this position, he wasn't about to lose the advantage. He held his finger on the button and was delighted when he saw the bomber go down and burst into flames.

Nigel Rose, who was following Babbage, also took aim on one of the bombers, having got himself into a good position whereby it was virtually impossible to miss - only to find that he had used up all his ammunition. He promptly returned to base, defenceless against further attack.

The German aircraft that had flown rather cockily across the Channel a short while ago were now in almost total disarray and fleeing across the Channel, their tails between their legs. They had had a pretty rough late afternoon and wouldn't forget it in a hurry. The were certainly not returning with the same buoyant attitude they had enjoyed when flying across the sea towards England. Many of their comrades would not be returning at all.

Gradually all the aircraft of the various squadrons that had taken part made off to their bases. The Spitfires of 602 returned to Westhampnett, their pilots exhausted but at the same time very excited. They were telling their stories to members of the ground staff even before they had climbed out of their cockpits, let alone reported to the intelligence officer.

This had certainly been the most successful combat the squadron had yet taken part in. They soon made out their 'combat reports' for Henry Grazebrook and, the official business over, made their way over to the mess for a well deserved pint. They knew, as history would confirm, that they had just won a very important battle.

Later reports showed that Tangmere's 17 Squadron had lost two Hurricanes. The aircraft of S/Ldr Williams had its port mainplane shot off in a head-on attack with a Bf 110. It crashed into the sea, the pilot missing. A second Hurricane was shot down, the pilot, F/Lt. Bayne, baling out into the sea and being rescued unhurt.

Exeter's 87 Squadron lost one Hurricane when Sergeant Wakeling's machine was shot down in flames just outside Dorchester and he was killed.

Warmwell's 152 Squadron lost two Spitfires, with both pilots missing.

213 Squadron, also based at Warmwell lost three Hurricanes, one of them managing to force-land back at base, the pilot unhurt. Another failed to return from combat, the pilot reported as missing. The third, flown by Pilot Officer Philippart was believed to have been shot down into the sea by Hptmn. Mayer of 1/JG53 off Portland. The pilot baled out over the sea and his body was washed ashore on August 28.

602 Squadron lost two Spitfires and 609 Squadron, from Warmwell, had two Spitfires badly damaged, although both made it back to their base. One pilot suffered a slight injury to his arm, while the other was unhurt.

The German losses included six Bf 110s and two Bf109s. A Junkers Ju88 crash-landed at Cherbourg, two crew members wounded. Many other aircraft were damaged, some making it back to their bases while others were believed to have crashed into the sea.

Paddy Barthropp remembers . . .

(Taken from the book 'The Battle of Britain' by Richard Townsend Bickers)

'On August 21 volunteers were called for to fly Spitfires. Having flown biplanes and Lysanders over the past year, I was pleased to have a go in something with a little more glamour and power attached to it. The Spitfire has been described as the best fighter aircraft of World War II and I wouldn't disagree, except to say that the narrow undercarriage and the early hydraulic system took some getting used to. The latter necessitated pumping the hydraulics manually and, during a hasty take off, gave rise to some hairy moments.

Having flown Spits from Mk1s to (later) Mk 24s I can say that the Spitfire was the most beautiful machine ever invented. I used to talk to mine all the time - "Keep going'!"and so on - and it almost talked back to me. '

'As little 'John Wayne's' I am certain we had no idea how tricky things really were at that period. All the rubbish about the 'Big Wings' as defined by Douglas Bader was a complete mystery to us, and still is. To assemble three squadrons in the air, a total of thirty-six aircraft, form into a wing and then direct it towards the enemy, took far too long as the Huns were only just across the Channel, a mere twenty miles away. So what he was going on about I really don't know.'

'The Battle of Britain was a great period to have lived through, but I often wonder what would have happened if the German fighter ace Adolph Galland and his merry men had had long range jettison tanks fitted to their aircraft to allow them rather more than fifteen minutes' combat time over London.

Together with superior numbers this would certainly have given them an even greater advantage, and the outcome of the Battle of Britain might have been very different.

The momentous aerial combat fought in the summer of 1940 was won by the inspiring leadership of Commander-in-Chief Fighter Command, Lord Dowding. His foresight in refusing to send futher fighter squadrons to France against the wishes of Winston Churchill and his military advisers gave Britain the resources and breathing space to continue the war until victory was achieved.'

August 26

This day was to see the very last mass daylight raid by German bombers - and once again the pilots of 602 Squadron would be right in the forefront of the battle.

During a leisurely morning of reading books and writing letters home Hector MacLean instructed Mickey Mount that he would be 'A' Flight Commander for the morning, as MacLean wished to organise the cutting of slit-trenches among the trees between the airfield and the public part of the area. This would give some protection against surprise low-level air attacks on the airfield.

It was part way through the morning that a car arrived, and the staff as a whole cast an eye upon the visitor who had arrived unannounced.

'Flight Lieutenant Macintosh, sir,' he reported to Sandy Johnstone.

'Ah, my new ground defence adviser,' came the response. 'Good! There's plenty for you to do.'

Macintosh had a florid complexion and a chest full of World War One medals. He was a very even tempered character, with a good sense of humour - which he needed, since he had to put up with a lot of stupid remarks. He had been a flight sergeant engineer, and was very knowledgeable about the Merlin engine. Indeed, he knew more about the engine than any other officer on the station. He was soon out examining the perimeter area.

As lunch time approached yet more visitors arrived. Captain Broome from Vickers had brought his wife along at Sandy's invitation. No sooner had the pilots begun to enjoy what seemed a promising social event, however, than their enjoyment was cut short. The Tangmere controller, David Lloyd, was alerted to the fact that a large German force had been assembled over France, and the telephone at Westhampnett immediately jangled into life: 'Scramble, scramble!'

Lloyd had alerted a number of squadrons early, giving them time to climb high and await the incoming bombers and their escorts. 602 were positioned a thousand feet above the estimated height of the German bombers. Two large formations were spotted some distance away, heading for the English coastline. In the first were more than thirty Heinkel He 111s of 1/KG55, 4/KG55 and 5/KG55, while the second formation, targetting Portsmouth dockyards, was made up of Dornier Do 17s (the flying pencils) and had a Messerschmitt escort including those from 2/JG2.

Combat would take place at a height of 15,000 feet, but Sandy Johnstone searched the skies in vain for the fighter escorts Thinking this strange, he gave the command and led the squadron down, line astern. Hector MacLean was leading 'A' Flight with Donald Jack tucked in behind, heading straight for the bombers. The Germans saw them only at the last minute, and then through the headphones of the 602 pilots came the words 'Schpitfeuren ! Schpitfeuren!' in a shrieking voice, immediately joined by another. For a moment Johnstone thought his pilots were fooling about, and he was on the point of reprimanding them when he realised that the voices were genuinely German: by a freak of the radio waves, the German bomber pilots were tuned into the very same frequency as the Spitfires.

The bombers were now at panic stations as the Hurricanes of 43 Squadron (Tangmere) joined in. Soon the air waves were filled with a Babel of English and German voices, hunter and hunted, twisted and turned. Some of the bombers, desperately trying to escape, released their bombs harmlessly into the sea - they had had enough and just wanted to get back across the Channel and head for home. Others weren't to get that chance.

Sandy Johnstone picked out the Heinkel leader of the group, who was still heading in towards his target, took aim and fired. To his amazement the Heinkel just behind the leader blew up, the aircraft shot apart and falling in blazing pieces. The leader had turned and was soon out over the sea. Sandy, thinking that he might have hit it as well, followed the Heinkel and fired his few remaining bullets into the fleeing aircraft.

Ginger Whall was also in the action, twisting and turning to avoid the Messerschmitt escort which had belatedly appeared and was attempting to protect the bombers. He at last got into a position where he could attack one of the Heinkels - one from 4/KG55, flown by Lt. Metzger. He struck it almost broadside, and it began to trail smoke and was soon on its way down. He followed it down, expecting to see the crew bale out. The pilot had been wounded during Whall's attack, but he fought to land his plane safely, unaware that his crewmen were already either dead or dying. Bleeding badly from a shoulder wound, and praying that the Spitfire wouldn't attack again, he eased the large German bomber down and down, managing to land it partly in the sea and partly on the beach at East Wittering. Lt. Metzger was taken to hospital and spent the rest of the war in captivity.

Ellis Aries was one of the youngest and most inexperienced 602 pilots. He had first flown operationally on the day that Tangmere was attacked ten days before. Now he saw a German aircraft lining up for an attack and, realising that he was a sitting duck, rolled away into the clouds and safety. As he came out of the clouds he was aware in the same instant of Portland Bill down below him and of one of the German bombers right in front. Guns blazing, he went in for his first kill. His bullets tore along the fuselage and the bomber went straight down. 'I've got one, I've got one!' he shouted over the R/T.

By now the Bf 109s were involved in a desperate struggle with the Spitfires and Hurricanes, the odds being 6-to-1 in the Germans' favour. Over Portsmouth a Heinkel He 111 got in a burst of gunfire as a Hurricane came in head-on, the fighter quickly bursting into flames. Pilot Officer North baled out with a head and shoulder wound. Another Hurricane was tangling with a Bf 109 of 2/JG2 and getting the better of it: the pilot, Oblt. Griesbach, just managed to bale out before the aircraft started its death spin. The combat was intense.

Another Bf 109 was hit and crashed: the pilot, either dead or unconscious, went down with his plane. In another part of the sky a Heinkel He 111 was frantically defending itself against the onslaught of the British fighters. A Hurricane was hit, bursting into flames. Pilot Officer Lane, having great difficulty in releasing the cockpit catch as the flames engulfed him, was wounded and badly burned, but eventually baled out and was taken to hospital. A Hurricane flown by Pilot Officer Charles Woods-Scawen suffered serious damage during the combat and was forced to leave the battle, returning to base: he was unhurt. Almost at the same time, a Spitfire of 234 Squadron was hit and had to force-land near East Grinstead.

Two other damaged Hurricanes returned to Tangmere, one pilot wounded. The Heinkel that had shot down the Hurricane in the frontal attack was in turn shot down. Another crashed at Waterlooville: one of the crew baled out but was too low and was killed. Yet another went down at Wick, the crew being captured.

Cyril Babbage was engaged with one of a pair of Bf 109s that had been after young Aries. As he turned in the tightest of circles, finger poised, the Bf 109 suddenly appeared in his sights. A short burst and the Messerschmitt rolled over and went spinning down. Babbage watched in order to claim a 'kill', and was then himself attacked by a pair of Bf 109s. He had committed the biggest sin - allowing his concentration to lapse for a vital split second.

He knew instantly that he was in trouble. His controls had gone, shot away by Hptmn. Mayer of 1/JG 53, and he was going down over the sea south east of Selsey Bill, his speed gathering. As he prepared to escape, the Spitfire started to twist, making it more difficult to get out. He released the canopy and the other tubes and cords - there was a lot to do in a very short time - and then he was out and drifting down towards the sea. He was picked up with slight injuries and brought ashore (see p. 3) at Bognor Regis before being taken to hospital. Meanwhile the Spitfire was quickly into a series of rolls, spinning into the sea, and sinking almost immediately.

As Babbage drifted down, Hector MacLean watched the remainder of the Heinkels turn for home. The word 'cowards' ran through his brain, and he remembered

All's well that ends well. Smiles all round as Cyril Babbage is rescued from the sea.

the bombs that had been dropped on a cinema at Portsmouth a few days earlier, killing a large number of children at a matinée. He was some way behind the retreating planes, but knew that he still had at least half of his ammunition left. Accelerating southwards towards France, he was soon within firing distance of a formation of about a dozen Heinkels. The German leaders, he knew, were good at navigation. If possible he should attack the leading aircraft, the front runner. He flew alongside the whole formation, with eyes only for the leader - it had become almost an obsession to get him.

'Wait, wait!' he urged himself, his finger poised. 'Now!'

He pushed the button and, seeing his bullets find their mark, gleefully exclaimed 'Got him!'

The bomber was trailing smoke by the time the French coast was in

Saviour of the skies. One of the 602 Spitfires at Westhampnett in the summer of 1940.

view and MacLean, job done, thought about turning for home. He never saw the Bf 109 flown by Lt. Zeis of 1/JG53, who opened up with his cannons, hitting the Spitfire. The aircraft lurched from port to starboard and then again to port, this time quite violently,the erratic motion accompanied by a number of loud bangs. He instantly felt a searing pain in his leg and saw that the German aircraft was coming in again to finish him off. Just managing to correct the Spitfire in time as the Bf 109 shot past, he knew that - all his ammunition spent - all he could do was avoid the German aircraft as best he could. Fortunately for him the German fighter was too low on fuel to continue the attack, and it headed off to France, quickly catching up with the retreating Heinkels.

Maclean glanced around and found that he was alone in the sky. He gently eased his Spitfire around and, looking down at the sea, wondered whether he would be able to make it back to base. The pain in his leg was increasing and he began to slip forward in his seat, nauseous and almost unconscious. He took deep breaths in order to clear his head. He thought about baling out, but realised that, with his injury, he probably wouldn't make it, especially going into the sea. He decided to stick to the task of trying to get the aircraft back to base, somehow. Certainly if he met another German fighter he was done for.

Further and further he flew back across the Channel, gritting his teeth in pain, not sure how much more he could endure. By the time he saw the English coastline there was little control in the aircraft, but he pushed the stick forward and felt the Spitfire respond. The elevator cable could only be hanging by a thread, he knew, and it was impossible to know whether there was sufficient control to execute a landing.

He was just a few hundred yards from land now: 'Come on, come on!'. So close to home, he glanced down for the first time at his legs. There were signs of blood on the clothing of his left one, but the right one was in a terrible mess. During the attack by the Messerschmitt 109, a cannon shell had entered the cockpit and exploded immediately behind his right boot. His foot had been severed from his leg, the blood still pumping furiously from the wound. Aware that he could bleed to death before help came, he turned the oxygen full on. The landfall he had just seen was on the Isle of Wight rather than the mainland. He passed over Portsmouth, turning eastwards, and dropped to about 500 feet.

'Come on,' he muttered to himself. 'Nearly there.'

With his uninjured foot he tried the rudder. Nothing: the cable had been shot away during the attack. The pain he was suffering swamped his thoughts, but he knew that he was in serious trouble and in danger of passing out. Tangmere would be the first airfield he would come to, and he made for it in preference to his home base at Westhampnett. Two long miles to go.

He came in from the south-west corner, over the trees, very low, prepared for a belly landing. The Spitfire hit the ground, bounced several times - each time increasing his agony - and at last came to a standstill. He reached for the canopy catch.

By the time the fire and ambulance vehicles reached him, MacLean was out of his cockpit and lying on the ground, his right leg propped up on the back of the wing. Still conscious, he gave vent to his feelings, directing a long line of highly descriptive words at the emergency services for the time they had taken. He was gently placed on a stretcher with a tourniquet applied to his leg, and was about to be carried to the ambulance when he asked one of the medical orderlies to fetch his boot from the cockpit, explaining that they were a brand new pair.

The orderly hurried to the badly damaged Spitfire and, climbing on the wing, reached down into the cockpit. When he saw a boot with a severed foot inside it, he promptly fainted, slipping off the wing and falling to the ground. He received medical attention and was taken away in the ambulance alongside Maclean.

Meanwhile Donald Jack had been on top form, diving in here there and everywhere, having shots at numerous German bombers. As far as he knew, none had gone down, but several were going home with his bullets in them. He continued to use his guns until at last his ammunition was spent. He returned to Westhampnett, his aircraft being quickly re-fuelled and re-armed, and within twenty minutes it was passed as ready for the next sortie.

An hour later he was up again, with Paul Webb as his wingman. The Tangmere controller had seen a single aircraft in the Isle of Wight area and thought that it might be a 'nuisance' raider. After a brief search they found their target, a Heinkel He 59 - a German seaplane. These were more elderly aircraft, used to rescue downed German pilots, and in the Dover area they were painted with a red cross and were not attacked by the British fighters. Apart from their rescue duties, however, they were also used to report on British shipping - the direction and other details they gave often culminated in an attack by the Luftwaffe - and this one was in full wartime camouflage. After a brief exchange of words between the two Spitfires, Webb spent his ammunition in an attacking dive on the Heinkel and saw the aircraft go down and crash in the sea

The pilots of 43 Squadron, based at Tangmere, had not come out of the battle too well, losing six Hurricanes, two of which returned to base damaged but with the pilots uninjured. Two of the other pilots were forced to bale out, wounded, while the two remaining aircraft managed to return to base, but with badly wounded pilots, one suffering serious burns.

The German losses were, however, greater: three Messerschmitts and seven Heinkels of KG55 shot down, a number of the crews losing their lives. There were a number of other German aircraft shot down but there is insufficient evidence to link them with this combat. It later transpired that a number of Heinkel He 111s had been badly damaged, barely making it across the Channel and crash-landing at various places, among them Le Havre, Dreux and Cherbourg. Another crashed into the Channel, close to the French coastline ,and all the crew were rescued.

• Sandy Johnstone and Doc. Willey visted Hector MacLean in the Royal West Sussex Hospital. He was sitting up in bed, reading, his head cut, his face a reddish mauve colour around the eyes.

'What the hell happened to you?' Sandy asked.

'Hit my head on the reflector when I landed.' he replied.

On his arrival at the hospital the doctors had made a quick assessment of his injuries and had amputated his right leg below the knee.

'I swear my right foot is itching,' Hector told his visitors with a grin, chirply despite it all. As they left, he called out: 'Losing a leg is one way of getting some leave!' and resumed his reading.

August 31

A thick haze shrouded the Channel on the morning of Saturday August 31, and the pilots were taking every advantage to relax, some in arm chairs, others outside on the grass. Their mood had been darkened by the news of the serious injuries sustained by the commanding officer of 43 Squadron, Squadron Leader John 'Tubby' Badger, DFC, a personal friend of Sandy's. He had been shot down in combat with Bf 109s over Kent the previous afternoon and had crash-landed. Sandy, suffering from a stomach bug and so off flying for a day or two, was making arrangments to visit him in hospital. Findlay Boyd would be in charge if the squadron was called for combat.

Just before 6pm many of the pilots were in the mess, although they were in the 'ready' situation, when the message came: 'German Bombers approaching Kent; Villa Squadron scramble!' Within two minutes the Merlin engines had burst into life and the trolley jacks were removed. With Findlay Boyd in the lead, the eleven Spitfires were soon pointing their noses eastwards, joined by 17 Squadron from Tangmere.

As they approached Biggin Hill they saw the German bombers, two large formations of Dornier Do 17s, commonly known as 'flying pencils' because of their narrow fuselages. These were from KG2. There was also a number of Bf 109s interspersed with the bombers - a very unusual sight as they were normally separated, with the fighters flying above or behind as escorts.

Other squadrons had been directed to the same area, and these included the Spitfires of 72 and 222 Squadrons from Biggin Hill and Hornchurch as well as the Hurricanes of 17 and 79 Squadrons, these coming from Tangmere and Biggin Hill respectively. The Hurricanes of 85 Squadron based at Croydon were also involved.

Findlay Boyd led 602 high above the bomber formations looking for other Bf 109 escorts. He found them, but what he didn't expect were the Junkers Ju 88s with them. There was no time for reflection, however. Boyd's voice came over the R/T: 'Villa ready, right, Tally Ho.' The squadron went straight into the middle of them, each pilot selecting a victim. Proctor, guns blazing, got in a perfect shot and watched the German fighter blow up. Then Dougie Elcombe claimed a 'kill' as his guns blasted a Bf 109 out of the skies, the aircraft going down almost vertically. The pilot managing to bale out, his parachute billowing out in the last of the evening sunlight. Back and forth across the Kent country-side the Spitfires and Hurricanes went, shooting the German aircraft down one after another.

Moody and Coverley both struck home on the German planes but were only able to claim a 'damaged' as they lost sight of them in the melée. One of the Hurricanes from 17 Squadron was involved in combat with a Bf 109 over

Maidstone, each firing at the other simultaneously, and both aircraft went down - the Hurricane force-landing at Yalding with the pilot, Sergeant Steward, unhurt. Then a Dornier Do 17 of 2/KG76 was hit and started to go down with black smoke trailing. It crashed at Newchurch, all the crew being taken prisoner. Next was a Bf 109, shot down by Pilot Officer Millington of 79 Squadron in his Hurricane, the German fighter crashing in flames at Lydd Ranges. The pilot was captured, badly burned.

And then, quite incredibly and as if someone had waved a magic wand, the German aircraft had gone - every one of them had disappeared. It was time to go home.

With Boyd leading the way they headed westwards, but they had got only a short way towards base when the voice of Elcombe came over the R/T. He reported that his temperature gauge was rising, and a fellow pilot observed that there was a glycol stream coming from Elcombe's aircraft. He was given the all clear to fall out from the formation, and he landed at Ford Naval Air Station. The aircraft had suffered minor damage, but Elcombe was uninjured. The aircraft was later repaired and put back in service.

On the occasion of this sortie the Bf 109s of JG26 were led by Major Galland, the German flying Ace and Commander of JG26. This was his third sortie of the day. The target was Hornchurch airfield, this being on the strict instructions of Generalfeldmarschall Kesselring. The bombers were from KG76.The third Gruppe flew a detached escort while the Bf.109s flew as 'close' escorts. Galland later stated that he and his third Gruppe were engaged in combat continuously from the English coast to the target area and back again. They claimed nine British aircraft shot down, but this was wide of the mark. However, what was agreed was that the fighting on this day was especially fierce. Major Galland claimed to have shot down a Spitfire over Gravesend. This was confirmed, giving him his 26th 'kill', with a Hurricane, shot down over Maidstone becoming his 27th.

Meanwhile, Oblt. Sprick, the 8 Gruppe commander, claimed two 85 Squadron Hurricanes shot down over Folkestone, although it is believed that both these aircraft, although damaged, managed to get back to their base at Croydon with their pilots uninjured.

Battle of Britain – Phase 4

September 7 – 30

*T*he German High Command was at this time very concerned about its lack of air superiority. Its timetable for the invasion of Britain was behind schedule because of the RAF's resistance during the dogfights of August, and victory now seemed no closer than it had been a month previously. Indeed, during the period between August 24 and September 6 the known German losses amounted to no fewer than 107 bombers and two Stuka dive-bombers.

For two months the Luftwaffe had tried just about everything to bring the main Fighter Command aircraft into a battle which would surely be won by the numerical superiority of the Bf 109s and Bf 110s.

From the very beginning there were many in the Luftwaffe Command who thought that only heavy daylight bombing of London and other selected British towns and cities would achieve the desired results. Consistent bombing would crack the morale of the British people until they begged for peace. Hitler, however, had different ideas and forbade these attacks, believing that Britain would soon sue for peace in any case.

This policy would soon change, thanks to the German Air Force. During the night of August 25 a number of bombs had been accidentally dropped on central London, in the main due to bad navigation. This incident goaded the RAF to bomb Berlin in retaliation. Although little damage was caused, Hitler was furious: how dare anyone bomb the German capital? Having conquered most of Europe, he found it extremely embarrassing to have the RAF aircraft flying over German soil and dropping bombs on Berlin night after night before returning to England practically unscathed.

On August 31 the Luftwaffe Command issued preliminary orders for a daylight reprisal raid on London, and two days later the plans were laid: London would be bombed by day and night. These plans failed to detract from the many heated arguments between Sperle and Kesselring over the RAF strength, the latter winning the day on a theory that Fighter Command was almost finished.

The Luftwaffe Command strongly believed that the numerous attacks on airfields stretching from the southern counties up to and around London had paved the way for a systematic 24-hour bombing of London. The plans were made and finalised, and September 7 was announced as the date for the commencement of the bombardment of the city. Hitler personally signed the order on September 2 for the reprisal raids to start.

In Britain, RAF Command had no idea of this change of tactics. They were, understandably, more concerned about defending the airfields.

The position for the fighter squadrons was grim at best, as their losses were increasing. Between August 24 and September 6 the RAF losses were simply staggering: 295 fighter aircraft had been totally destroyed and another 171 badly damaged. Worst still was the fact that 103 pilots had been killed or posted as missing, with another 128 pilots wounded and out of the air. In a single week 616 Squadron had lost a dozen aircraft and five pilots; 603, newly arrived in 11 Group, 16 aircraft and 12 pilots; and 253 squadron, based at Kenley, 13 Hurricanes and nine pilots.

During the month of August around 260 pilots passed through the flying training schools, but during the same period pilot casualties amounted to just over 300. The experienced pilot was by now like gold dust, and the heavy losses meant that the squadrons were relying on inexperienced and untried young men who, in the early stages at least, would be vulnerable.

A report by Fighter Command on September 12 stated that, contrary to general belief and official reports, the enemy's bombing attacks by day had done extensive damage to five forward aerodromes and also to six out of seven sector stations. The damage to forward aerodromes was so severe that Manston and Lympne were totally unfit for fighters for several days. Biggin Hill was so heavily damaged that only one squadron could operate from its airfield, the remaining two squadrons having to be placed under the control of adjacent sectors for over a week. The report continued that if the enemy continued the heavy attacks to the adjacent sectors, knocking out their operations rooms or telephone communications, the fighter defences of London would be in a powerless state during the last critical phase, and unopposed heavy attacks would be directed against the capital.

Squadrons from the front line were now temporarily moved back, to be replaced by rested squadrons.

September 7

*A*ll in all, Saturday September 7 was a bad day, not only for 602 but for London, as this turned out to be the first day of the Blitz. Hitler had now changed tactics, moving from attacking the RAF airfields to terrorising the populace. The bombing of the capital continued day and night, non-stop.

Many Londoners took to the shelters by night, but then in the mornings would make their way to work for a very full day. Come the night, the cycle would continue all over again, seemingly endlessly.

The fighter squadrons were kept very busy, especially those of 11 Group, and on this day the main action would take place over the Kent countryside, stretching the length and breadth of the county and spilling out above Sussex.

At Westhampnett there had been a few new pilots joining the squadron during the past couple of days. These included 'Nuts' Niven, Pedro Hanbury and Roy Payne. They were all good flyers, but they needed to be trained on Spitfires.

Just before two in the afternoon the squadron was called to 'readiness', and shortly afterwards two visitors arrived: Group Captain Jack Boret, the C.O. of Tangmere, and the Chief of Air staff, Sir Cyril Newall. They had only been at the airfield a matter of minutes when the squadron was ordered to patrol Hawkinge at 'Angels 15' (15,000ft). The hastiest of farewells and the pilots were off.

The headstone at Scarborough to Flying Officer Bill Coverley, mortally wounded in combat on this day.

The Hurricanes of Tangmere had also been scrambled, and 602's Spitfires caught up with them before they reached Kent. It had been rather a hot morning, and there was a heat haze all the way up. As they emerged through the heat haze the pilots nearly jumped out of their cockpits. The German aircraft were already there - hundreds of them, row upon row of bombers, all heading for London. Immediately identified were Junkers Ju 88s Heinkel He 111s, Dornier Do 17s and escorts of Bf 109s and Bf 110s. Wave after wave were coming in, stretching as far as the eye could see. Sandy Johnstone, amazed by the sheer volume of enemy aircraft, knew this would be an exceptional battle.

Several squadrons were scrambled to attack this massive force, including Spitfires and Hurricanes from 43, 79, 111,222, 234, 249 and 609 Squadrons.

The German fighters saw the Spitfires and Hurricanes and came straight in, diving down from above. It was like a race when the flag is dropped. Aircraft were diving, twisting and turning, engines screaming, speeds increasing. It was difficult to pinpoint each individual combat. The battlefield stretched for many miles, right across London and the southern part of Essex.

A Hurricane of 43 Squadron was one of the first to be hit, almost at once bursting into flames: the pilot was out quickly, landing safely near Ashford, but the aircraft twisted over and over before crashing into the ground. Another Hurricane went down. This time the pilot didn't get out, and was killed. Sandy Johnstone quickly gave up striving for an overview and concentrated on getting at the bombers. He saw a plane, close to him get shot down, and a Bf110 passed in front of him before he could draw a bead on it. He was trying to listen over the radio, but the noise and shouting of the dozens of pilots taking part in this combat was deafening, and most of the time they were indecipherable, with just the odd word being understood.

Someone had hit a Dornier. Its port mainplane missing, it was spinning out of control, the parachutes of the crew billowing out as they sailed down - one of these, a rather skinny German, holding on to his 'chute cords tightly, his eyes dripping fear.

The Spitfires of the squadron were spread far and wide.The combat had been taking place for quite some while yet, incredibly, the German bombers were still coming in across the Channel, filling the skies for as far as could be seen. A Spitfire hit one of the Heinkels. Its bullets could be seen hitting the whole length of the fuselage before the massive bomber made two turns, flipped over and plummeted.

Now the failing evening sun glinted on open parachutes wafting down, giving an eerie glow. It was an unwritten law that pilots who had baled out were not to be attacked, although there were cases where it happened.

Meanwhile the battle continued. Pedro Hanbury attacked a Dornier Do 17. Although he believed he had done enough to shoot it down, he was hit by return fire, causing damage to his radiator. The Spitfire was soon beginning to overheat, so he informed his leader and carefully made his way back to base. He was unhurt, and the Spitfire was able to be repaired in a short time.

Ellis Aries attacked another Dornier Do 17 over Biggin Hill and he, too, was hit by return fire, his Spitfire quickly trailing black smoke which he could see in his mirror. With damage to the Glycol tank and a heaviness in his controls, he started to descend. As he lost altitude he made out a suitable field to the west of Wrotham and close to the A20, and there he landed safely. Later his Spitfire was removed and repaired.

There was a moment of humour in this death or die struggle. A young pilot on the radio was heard to exclaim in an excited voice: 'Bloody hell, I've just shot down Goering!' - and there, in the midst of this massive battle, was a portly German floating down to earth, dangling at the end of his parachute with his arms held high in a gesture of surrender. Smiles and laughter all round.

Another pilot, Harry Moody, handsome and reserved, was soon very much involved in this heady battle. He was heard to have exclaimed at one point, having seen the massive German armada: 'Jesus Christ, it's the whole of the Luftwaffe.' Soon afterwards, while involved in combat somewhere over Biggin Hill, he disappeared. No trace of him or his Spitfire No. X4256 was ever found. In fact no one could recall seeing what happened to him.

Yet another pilot was to lose his life in this particular air battle. Flying Officer Bill Coverley, a quiet and dedicated young man flying Spitfire N3198 , had attacked a Bf 109, although it wasn't ascertained whether he had achieved a 'kill'. He in turn was attacked, his aircraft seen hurtling down in flames over the Biggin Hill area.

The flames were coming from the cockpit area, and his colleagues were urging him to get out before it was too late. After a struggle he managed to open the cockpit hood and, though badly burned, to bale

Pedro Hanbury. This wasn't to be his day.

out. His parachute opened and was seen close to landing, while his Spitfire crashed in a big ball of flames at Fosters Farm near Tonbridge, the remains being scattered over a wide area. Coverley's body was found a week later, very badly burned, in the top of a tall tree.

Many other allied Spitfires and Hurricanes were either damaged or shot down in this very fierce battle but it was deemed a victory for the pilots of Fighter Command as a large number of German bombers and fighters were shot down, failing to make their targets.

The Spitfires of 602 were soon over their base again at Westhampnett and one by one landed safely. The pilots jumped out of their cockpits, tired but quite elated at the late afternoon's work, although on this occasion there would be no smiles or laughter: two of their kind were missing. The loss of Harry Moody and Bill Coverley had put a dampener on the aftermath of a battle in which the squadron had acquitted themselves admirably.

The final totals of the various squadrons' losses were high. 43 squadron had lost three Hurricanes with two pilots killed. 79 had one Hurricane damaged but with no pilot injuries. Another hurricane was lost, this one from 111 Squadron: the pilot baled out slightly hurt. 222 Squadron from Hornchurch had two Spitfires damaged. 234 Squadron lost two Spitfires together with their pilots, both being killed. The worst losses were suffered by 249 squadron, based at North Weald. They lost six Hurricanes with one pilot killed and three wounded: one of these Hurricanes, having attacked a Dornier, was believed to have been hit by 'friendly' AA fire. 609 Squadron had three Spitfires hit and damaged, but they landed safely with no injuries to the pilots.

German records show that on this day almost a thousand aircraft crossed the Channel. They were stepped from 14,000 feet to 23,000 feet and covered an area of 800 square miles. One of the German fighters shot down was a Bf 109E - 4, Number 5385 of JG26, which had been escorting the Junkers Ju 88's of KG30. This aircraft force-landed near Pluckley, Kent. The pilot, Oblt. Hans Krug, was captured unhurt, spending the remaining years as a prisoner of war. The downing of this aircraft gave the RAF a useful early look at a Bf 109E - 4 bomber.

It is not possible to ascertain fully the German losses as a number ditched in the Channel, while others crashed after reaching the French coast, and the German records do not give sufficiently full details. However, it is known that all types of German aircraft on this raid were shot down, including Dornier Do. 17s, Heinkel He 111s, Junker Ju 88s, Bf 110s and Bf 109s.

• On the Sunday morning, two of Harry Moody's closest colleagues sat down in the local church. They were not regular churchgoers, but they felt they should attend on this day. The vicar noticed them sitting together at the end of one of the pews. In a quiet and sensitive voice he read from Psalm 63: 'In the shadow of thy wings, I sing for joy. My soul clings to thee, thy right hand upholds me, but those who seek to destroy my life shall go down into the depths of the earth; they shall be given over to the power of the sword, they shall be prey for jackals. But the King shall rejoice in God; all who swear by Him shall glory; for the mouths of liars will be stopped.'

They stepped out into the hazy September sun feeling glad that they had spent a little time there.

September 9

The weather had changed dramatically - rain and thunder - and their mood matched it. Thoughts continually turned to the two missing pilots, Harry Moody and Roger Coverley, and deep down it was beginning to dawn on them that these two brave young pilots would never come back.

Some of the London bombing stories had seeped through to those at Westhampnett. One of the pilots remarked later: 'It wasn't easy, flying at 15 or 20,000 feet with the enemy trying to shoot you down, but it was far better than being on the streets at that time.' One of the most harrowing stories was of buses being blown up, with many people killed and injured - one bus almost disappearing into a large hole and another being blown halfway up a wall and almost into someone's bedroom.

September is often referred to as the fourth phase of the Battle of Britain but to the squadron, there was no difference. The Germans were still coming over to bomb a number of targets, in particular London. The 602 pilots were still being 'scrambled,' sometimes several times a day - just like the old days.

Today, however, lunch was taken without any interruptions, the new pilots beginning to wonder what all the fuss was about. They swapped news. Ginger Whall had been awarded the DFM, and Mickey Mount had been promoted to flight lieutenant: he was now to take over as 'A' Flight commander as Dunlop Urie was still recovering from the injuries he had recently sustained and would then be sent away for a rest.

Then the alarm sounded, and they were out of the door and running for their trusty Spitfires. The radar had tracked a large raid, and 602 would be joined by more squadrons when they reached their area.

Approaching Mayfield, they saw a fair- sized force of Dornier Do 17s being split up in utter confusion by 605, a squadron of Hurricanes from Croydon led

On standby. Members of 602 take a nap, awaiting the next call to action.

by Archie McKellar - one of our top fighter pilots, who had previously been with 602. More German bombers were a few miles behind: Heinkels He 111s and Junkers Ju 88s. About this time the Bf 109 escort aircraft came down at speed from a height of 30,000 feet. They had been waiting for the fighters to appear, and now the fighting was fast and furious. Spitfire bullets were hitting Hurricanes and vice versa as well as finding their intended targets. Sandy Johnstone and Pat Lyall attacked a Dornier Do 17 and watched with satisfaction as their bullets crashed into the German bomber. Almost immediately the crew baled out, leaving the aircraft to crash in north Sussex. The parachutes of the crew billowed out and they floated into captivity.

Sandy Johnstone didn't notice the Bf 109 on his tail, but just before the German could fire at him Pat Lyall saw his C.O.'s plight and managed to get his shot in first. The Bf 109 trailed smoke and, spinning like a top, crashed to earth. The action was manic.

About half past five, in combat over Croydon, two Hurricanes of 310 Squadron collided. One of them struck a Dornier, and both these aircraft crashed, the Hurricane at Woodmanstern in Surrey. F/Lt. Sinclair managed to bale out as his aircraft went out of control, and landed in a wood at Caterham, suffering a sprained ankle. Close to this wood, another Hurricane of 242 Squadron crashed, having been shot down by a combination of a Dornier and a Bf110: the pilot was killed.

Meanwhile, Jack Proctor had managed to get near enough to the bombers and let fly with his guns, hitting one of the Dorniers. He saw pieces of the aircraft fly off, but it didn't go down. He never got a second chance at it. Then there was a curse coming loud and clear over the R/T from Andy McDowall, as he missed his intended target, soon followed by a yelp of delight as his guns hit a Bf 109, blowing it to pieces, the pilot killed.

Not to be outdone, Ginger Whall downed one German bomber, the crew quickly escaping their stricken plane, and then had a go at another. He fired a two-second burst which missed, then got a little closer and tried again. This time he hit the fuselage just behind the wing and saw small pieces chip off. The bomber peeled away and disappeared from view.

Whall was looking for something else to attack, and had just set his sights on another bomber when he felt a judder which told him that he had been hit. With a German fighter now close behind him, he started to weave about, dropping lower and increasing his speed. When he looked in his mirror again the German fighter had gone, but his controls had been damaged. He eventually saw Arundel Castle a little way ahead of him and, selecting a field, managed to land his Spitfire with the wheels down. He suffered an injury to his neck but otherwise was unhurt. His aircraft was later repaired.

Newly promoted Paul Webb was probably one of the luckiest of the 602 pilots. His Spitfire had been badly damaged over Mayfield and, trailing smoke, was careering out of the battle. As he went down he was suddenly aware of three Bf 109s on his tail, ready to finish him off. The earth seemed to be rushing up to meet him as the 109s continued to rake his aircraft with fire. Time and time again he felt it shudder. Not only was the engine damaged so that he couldn't climb, but first his rudder control went, the cable and links shot through, and then his aileron controls were hit. Reduced to flying in a straight line, the enemy unable to miss, he was convinced that these were his last moments alive. He was so intent on controlling the plane that he was unaware that the Bf 109s had pulled out, obviously regarding him as a goner. His speed was far too fast, he was too low and, with no lateral control, he had no option but to throttle back, aim his sick Spitfire straight ahead, cross his fingers and pray.

The Spitfire, still hurtling too fast, cut through the tops of trees at Crocker Hill, Boxgrove. The foliage seemed to explode around the cockpit, and for a second or so his view disappeared. The propeller cut into the upper branches and, with two mighty crashing sounds, both wings broke clean away from the fuselage. The force of this impact certainly slowed the fuselage up but there was still enough force to keep it moving. The next second and the tail section broke off, and then the weight of the engine pulled the nose section down into the soft ground. Still the shattered remains refused to stop, however, continuing to move forward for another 50 yards or so before finally coming to a stop.

Several people had witnessed this horrible smash and went running forward, expecting to find the pilot dead, and probably mangled, in the cockpit. Removing the hood, however, they were amazed to find 'Webby' still semi-concious and cursing loudly (and thankfully) to himself. His injuries amounted to nothing more than a broken wrist, four broken fingers and a deep cut to his head. He was patched up and soon found himself back at Westhampnett, relating his incredible story.

A number of other Squadrons were involved in this battle, including 19, 66, 92 and 303 Squadrons.

19 Squadron, based at Duxford, had two Spitfires damaged but managed to return to base, their pilots unhurt.

66 Squadron, based at Kenley, had one Spitfire shot down during combat over East Grinstead, the pilot baling out slightly wounded.

92 Squadron had one Spitfire shot down: the pilot baled out badly burned. Another aircraft crash-landed near Rye, the pilot having shrapnel wounds to his legs. A third Spitfire, flown by Pilot Officer Allan Wright, just managed to return to base, badly damaged.

A Hurricane of 303 Squadron flown by Flight Sergeant Wunsche was involved in combat over Beachy Head, made landfall and crashed at Poynings, north of Brighton. The pilot baled out, landed near Devil's Dyke with slight burns and was admitted to hospital in Hove.

Two Hurricanes of 605 Squadron were hit by crossfire from Heinkels of KG53. One had the side of the cockpit shot away and was abandoned by the pilot, who suffered a hand injury. The other Hurricane was shot down over Farnborough and then collided with a Heinkel of Stab III/KG53, falling minus its starboard wing. The pilot was killed. The Heinkel He 111H-2 crashed at Chawton, near Alton, Hampshire. Three members of the crew were killed and two baled out and were captured.

A Bf 110C ditched in the sea about five miles off Newhaven, with one of the crew killed and the other captured.

A Junkers Ju 88A-2 was shot down and force-landed at Bannisters Farm, Barcombe, near Lewes. One crew member was killed and three others were captured. The aircraft burned out.

A Bf 109 crash landed near Storrington, while another came down at Mayfield and a third ditched in the sea about six miles off Newhaven: the pilot was captured.

A large number of other German aircraft were shot down in various parts of Kent and also over the Channel. Some, badly damaged, made it back to France. The Luftwaffe had been badly mauled by the British fighters on this day.

September 11

Today the targets were Portsmouth, Southampton and London. Come mid-afternoon the call to scramble was received as a large force from both Cherbourg and Seine Bay were approaching the Selsey Bill area and linking up. Soon after 602 and 213 took off, two other large German formations were sighted heading once more for London. The squadrons were now being stretched, but in the end would give a very good account of themselves. •

The enemy were soon sighted heading westwards towards Portsmouth, flying almost parallel to the coastline. The Hurricanes made a beeline for the bombers, while the Spitfires of 602 were more than happy to take care of the escort aircraft. It wasn't long before first one Bf 109 went down, soon followed by another. Cyril Babbage was once again in the thick of it. He attakced a Bf 110 with all guns blazing, but just in time the German aircraft managed to turn to port and suffered very minor damage. He then attacked Babbage, who quickly withdrew out of range.

Meanwhile one of the Hurricanes took care of a German bomber, which streamed smoke as it went down. FindlayBoyd selected a Bf 109 which turned tail, heading back towards the sea. To run away was useless, however, as Boyd's Spitfire soon got within range, and after a couple of quick squirts the Bf 109 crashed into the sea about five miles off Selsey Bill.

213 Squadron took out another of the bombers but, soon after, tragedy struck. A Hurricane of 213 Squadron, flown by Sgt Wojcicki, was shot down about a mile south of Selsey Bill, the pilot losing his life. Then another German aircraft went down, but this was followed soon afterwards by an attack on Stuart Rose's Spitfire: he managed to land back at base, but had been wounded.

The next Spitfire to get hit was Melvyn Sprague's. He had bravely attacked a Bf 110, but in doing so had been hit by return fire. He may have been wounded before he lost control and, his aircraft streaming black smoke, crashed into the sea.

Cyril Babbage also found himself in combat with the Bf 110s, and he was also hit, the Spitfire suffering severe damage to the starboard wing. He returned to base uninjured. The Hurricane of Flight Lieutenant Sing was damaged in the glycol and gravity petrol tank, and the pilot made a quick exit, landing unhurt.

As so often happened, the skies suddenly cleared of the German aircraft, two of which managed to limp across the Channel and crash-land on French soil. The remaining Spitfires and Hurricanes returned to their bases. This was to be the only action of the day.

Some of the bombers made it through to their target and bombed Portsmouth but, thanks to the interception by the Spitfires and Hurricanes, the damage was classed as 'nominal'.

The officers' mess at Westhampnett was again subdued. The loss of Melvyn Sprague was made even worse by the fact that he had only four days before returned from his honeymoon.

On the aircraft front the news was decidely gloomy. Having lost another Spitfire on this day, with two more damaged, they could now muster only five serviceable planes, while over at Tangmere the two Hurricane squadrons had only seven to fly between them. Urgent telephone calls had been going on for most of the day between Tangmere and RAF Command.

On the brighter side, the squadron was informed of two more awards: the Military Cross for Doc Willey and the Distinguished Flying Medal for Sandy Johnstone.

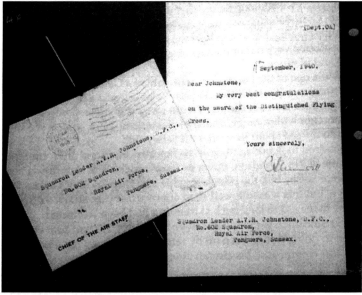

Good news among the bad. This is the letter informing Sandy Johnstone, 602's commanding officer, that he had been awarded the Distinguished Flying Medal.

Battle of Britain Day September 15, 1940

'There was a touch of mist in the air over southern England on the morning of 15th September. It cleared fairly quickly and the sun shone through clear and bright. It was excellent bombing weather.'

*A*t around 11 o'clock on the morning of Sunday, September 15 a large German formation was detected massing over Boulogne and Calais. The target, once again, was London. The attack was to be a repeat of the September 7 onslaught. The Luftwaffe commanders and air crew had doubts about the real value of these attacks, because their losses were mounting at quite an alarming rate. The difference this time was that their bombers were going to fly direct to London instead of engaging in diversionary attacks as had happened in the past - the object having been to disguise the real target.

The German bomber formation crossed the Channel at 15,000 feet, rising to 26,000 feet as it crossed the English coastline over Dungeness. The RAF squadrons were ready and waiting, and they immediately went into the attack - at first without 602. As more squadrons joined in, 602 were kept in readiness.

The squadron, together with 607 from Tangmere, were at last scrambled, but by the time they reached Mayfield, their target, the action had finished. This was young Paddy Barthropp's first sortie with 602, and he knew enough to realise that to be in the front line was going to be a tough job despite the damp squib of this early experience. The squadrons were soon back at base, settling down to grab a bite of lunch.

Their rest was short lived: at 2.15pm the dreaded telephone summoned them to scramble. They set course for the Kenley-Biggin Hill-Gravesend area. Again they were one of the last squadrons to be summoned, as they had been kept in reserve. This now meant that all squadrons within 11 Group were committed, with no reserves left. If needed, other squadrons would be called from the other groups.

As 602 with their 12 Spitfires were leaving Westhampnett, 609 Squadron from Middle Wallop (10 Group) were taking off with their 13 Spitfires to be vexed to the Brooklands - Kenley area.They sighted two formations of Dornier Do 17s and Heinkel He 111s over Edenbridge, Kent. 602 was led by Sandy Johnstone and, ever watchful, his eyes searched the sky for the escorting Bf 109s. At this time they weren't seen. He gave the order, and they went in to attack the

Dorniers, which were flying slightly higher than the Heinkels. They picked their targets and, gathering speed, they were soon down upon them. The German planes scattered as quickly as they could, but not before four Dorniers had gone down, three of them at least definite 'kills' The others jettisoned their bombs in a blind panic and were soon turning for home.

The Bf 109s and 110s were now on the scene, and once again the skies became a maelstrom of twisting and turning pieces of flying metal. Fighters and bombers all seemed to be firing at once, the sky a tracery of lead. First one aircraft would go down, then an opponent would fall. One parachute was followed by another, then another, and now there were several at once, the skies beginning to fill.

Pilot Officer Paddy Stephenson of 607 Squadron found two of the Dorniers coming straight for him. The closing speeds made it impossible for him to take any avoiding action: there wasn't even time to fire any shots at them. In the split second he had, he aimed his Hurricane at the very narrow gap between the two German bombers. Incredibly, he felt two bumps and muffled bangs as first one wing and then the other wing crashed into the Dorniers, and both went down out of control, the wings torn from their fuselages. Meanwhile, Paddy suddenly found himself in the bright clear sky - minus both of his own wings. He quickly baled out and what was left of his Hurricane crashed down to the ground. One of the Dorniers exploded in a wood near Goudhurst, Kent, the crew all killed. There are no details of the other one.

A little further away, a number of Dorniers were scattered by a single Hurricane in a head on attack. Above, a Bf 109 pilot, completely astonished by what he had just seen, lost his concentration and shot down his own section leader. He was then shot down by one of the Hurricanes.

Paddy Barthropp, on his first major sortie, knew that he was involved with something really historic, later making a note in his log book: 'Thousands of them'. He admitted later: 'I exhausted my ammunition, but God knows if I hit anything. When you are milling around, absolutely terrified, looking behind you and firing at something painted with Swastikas, it is difficult, if not impossible, to follow the progress of 'Harry the Hun' from 25,000 feet to the deck.'

Archie Lyall was one of the first to get at the Dorniers. His target made a run for it, dropping its bombs in an effort to increase speed. It became a race, a death race, as the Dornier, now picking up speed, headed for the Channel. They were some five miles north of St. Leonards when the Spitfire's bullets hit the German bomber. Coming back along the coast, Lyall attacked another Dornier near Beachy Head before heading back towards the Kent countryside.

As he re-joined the battle, 602 was racing alongside the bombers, damaging at least two more. Cyril Babbage also chased after a Dornier bomber, but was unable to get near enough to attack it until they reached Beachy Head. He hit the German plane with two bursts of fire, but his Spitfire was hit by return fire, severely damaging his engine. He knew that he wasn't going to make it back to base, so headed westwards along the coast and force-landed at Shoreham.

The whole of the action lasted just a few minutes, a very small part in a vast battle which filled the skies as far as anyone could see. The massive air armada stretched 70 miles back across the Channel, spreading across a nine- mile front five miles high. These measurements alone are massive and very difficult to imagine.

As the German bombers in the vanguard were being attacked and shot down, others were still crossing the Channel, their turn to come. A Dornier towards the front was attacked and shot down by a Spitfire of 609 Squadron. Trailing thick black smoke, it came down from a height of 22,000 feet. The Spitfire pilot watched but kept his distance, expecting the bomber to explode and break up at any moment.. In fact it crash-landed at Eighteen Pounder Farm at Westfield, near Hastings: one crew member baled out and was never found, while the others were captured.

By this time the 602 pilots found that their fuel was getting short and so Sandy ordered the squadron to return to base. It was a wonderful and majestic sight to see the Spitfires coming in to land at Westhampnett, the evening sunshine reflecting from their fuselages. They were soon parked in their dispersal units: incredibly there wasn't even a scratch on any of these aircraft. Paddy Barthropp made another entry in his diary: 'Still thousands of them.'

602 Squadron 'B'Flight, September/October, 1940. Left to right: Sgt Babbage DFM; Pilot Officer G. Fisher; F/Sgt Andy McDowall DFM and Bar; F/Lt. Donald Jack.

Back in the mess, the pilots listened to the BBC news on their wireless set. This was one of the few times when the place was unusually quiet. They were astonished to hear the BBC report that during this day the Luftwaffe had been given its most overwhelming beating. The announcer declared that they had suffered their largest loss of any one day, with 185 aircraft of all types confirmed as being shot down. This was, in fact, a gross exaggeration, the real score being in the region of 60 aircraft, but the true figure is astonishing enough. The RAF lost a total of 27 aircraft, with 13 pilots killed or missing.

This happened to be the third of the most critical days of the Battle of Britain, and ultimately the decisive one. The Luftwaffe had been determined to break both Fighter Command and the spirit of the civilian population by the scale of its attacks - attacks that were intended to engage the RAF's dwindling numbers of defending aircraft and pilots while raining an annihilating weight of bombs on London. The outcome, however, was not the overwhelming of Great Britain but the further frustration and final disillusionment of the Luftwaffe, which suffered its heaviest ever loss of aircraft and men.

The 602 pilots had good reason to remember this day. It wasn't evident at the time, but this was to be the last major daytime battle over Britain. The Germans would soon switch to night bombing, mounting only small fighter bomber raids by day - a pattern which was to continue for the rest of the year.

Many fighters and bombers from both sides were either shot down or badly

Sandy Johnstone landing at Westhampnett.

damaged on this day. The records show that Luftwaffe losses amounted to 83 while RAF losses were 64. (It is very difficult to quote correct numbers: these have been taken from *The Battle of Britain* by Dr. Price, a former aircrew member of the RAF who is renowned for his detailed research.)

Dense clouds saved many of the intended targets of the afternoon raids on London. Twenty Heinkels of BG 53 and 11 Dornier Do 17s of BG 3 had been meant to attack the Royal Victoria Docks, but switched to the West Ham area instead. The next attack by 27 Heinkels of BG 26 was similarly diverted from the West India Docks to bomb the Bromley-by-Bow gas works.

The final group, just minutes behind, were briefed to attack the Surrey Commercial Docks but instead bombed targets in South East London and Kent.

Sixty of the Luftwaffe crews were killed, 25 were reported missing, 30 were wounded and 63 were captured.

WHAT THEY SAID ABOUT BATTLE OF BRITAIN DAY

Winston Churchill, Britain's wartime prime minister:
'The 11 Group Operations Room was like a small theatre, about sixty feet across and with two storeys. We took our seats in the 'Dress Circle'. Below us was the large-scale map-table, around which perhaps twenty highly trained young men and women, with their telephone assistants, were assembled. Opposite to us, covering the entire wall where the theatre curtain would be, was a gigantic blackboard divided into six columns with electric light bulbs, for the six 11 Group fighter stations, each of their squadrons having a sub-column of its own, and also divided by lateral lines. Thus the lowest row of bulbs showed as they were lighted the squadrons that were 'standing by'.... The next row those at 'readiness'... then at 'available'.... Then those that had taken off, the next row those that had reported seeing the enemy, the next - with red lights - those that were in action, and the top row those which were returning home.'

Flying Officer Robert 'Bobby' Oxspring, 66 Squadron:
'Every squadron in 11 Group had intercepted, and at that moment I saw Douglas Bader's wing of five squadrons coming in from Duxford. This was the day when Goering had said to his fighters the RAF were down to their last 50 Spitfires. But they had run up against 23 squadrons for a start. When they were on their way in and then when they had got over London, with the Messerschmitt 109s running out of fuel, in comes Douglas Bader with 60 more fighters.'
[Bobby Oxspring was born in Sheffield on May 22, 1919, the son of a 1914-18 War fighter Ace. He joined 66 Squadron at Duxford after training in 1938.]

Like his father, he was to become an Ace. His record is impressive: 13 destroyed, one shared, two probables, 13 damaged and four V-1s destroyed. He was awarded the DFC in November 1940, a Bar in September 1942, a second Bar in February 1943 and later the AFC. He retired from the RAF as a Group Captain in 1968 and died in 1989.]

Squadron Leader Douglas Bader, 242 Squadron:

'This time, for a change, we outnumbered the Hun and, believe me, no more than eight got home from that party. At one time you could see planes going down on fire all over the place, and the sky seemed full of parachutes. It was sudden death that morning, for our fighters shot them to blazes.'

[Douglas Bader was probably the most widely known participant in the Battle of Britain, returning to flying after losing both his legs. (His story was told in the film Reach for the Sky.*) His war tally was 20 destroyed, four shared, six probables, one shared and 11 damaged.*

He left the RAF in February 1946, was awarded a CBE in 1956 and was knighted in 1976. He made his final flight at the controls on June 4, 1979, nearly 50 years after he had his first flight. He died in 1982.]

Sergeant Iain Hutchinson, 222 Squadron:

'They needed everyone they could find in the air on September 15. My squadron had taken off, but I didn't have a plane. My aircraft was unserviceable, I think, or maybe it was that I had been shot down the previous day and didn't have a replacement. I don't remember exactly. But I stole a plane from 41 squadron, which was also at Hornchurch, and went up with them. We did an attack on some bombers and then got split up. I was flying with another Spitfire - a friend of mine in 41 Squadron - watching the sky on my side. The next time I looked around my friend was gone and there was a Messerschmitt 109 in his place. I'm not sure what happened next, but I was shot down. It's not recorded in the official records because, not being in 41 Squadron, my name couldn't appear in its list of casualties.'

Pilot Officer Crelin 'Boggle' Bodie, 66 Squadron:

The morning of September 15 dawned - blue, cloudless sky, fine flying weather. It was Sunday - what of it? Hundreds of bombers and fighters swarmed across the Channel.

Our turn didn't come until about 11.30am, when we were ordered to patrol at 20,000 feet; off we went. I was in my usual position as 'weaver' flying alone 1.000 feet above the rest of the squadron, watching for attack from the rear or out of the sun. Soon we spotted a formation of Dorniers, and the squadron attacked. I followed, keeping a keen lookout behind, and wasn't surprised to see a dozen or more Bf 109s diving down on us.

By now the foremost people in the squadron were in amongst the Dorniers, so I told them about the 109s and engaged the nearest, but before I could get him in my sights I was fairly in the soup: they were all around me. They didn't do their job and protect the bombers but all went for me because I was on my own. I saw the squadron disappearing, dealing most effectively with the fleeing Dorniers, and realised that I was in no position to stay and play with a dozen Bf 109s. Several of them were on my tail, so I beat it straight down, flat out. I levelled out at 12,000 feet - that had shaken them off. I was all-alone. I called up the squadron on the radio, told 'em I was no longer with them, and beetled off to see what I could find patrolling a few miles south of London.

I saw a blob coming up from the south, and investigated. Boy! Oh boy! Twenty fat Dorniers, flying wing tip to wing tip, ack-ack all around. I was well ahead and above them, so I shoved the old throttle open, and dived at them head on. I picked the chappie who appeared to be leading the bunch, settled him in my sights and let him have it.

There isn't much time to muck about in a head on attack. I gave a short burst, then slid underneath his big black belly with only feet to spare, and flashed through the rest of the formation. I hadn't meant to cut it so close, and instinctively ducked as I saw wings, engines, cockpits and black crosses go streaking past my hood. I had reached about 450 mph in my dive, and heaved back on the stick. I blacked out completely as I went up and over in an enormous loop. My sight returned as I lost speed and the centrifugal force lessened. I was on my back, so I rolled over. The speed of dive and pullout had carried me up ahead of them for another attack. I saw that my first burst had taken effect; the leader had dropped away and to one side, and was turning back. The rest of the formation were wobbling about, and didn't seem to know quite what to do.

As I dived again, two Hurricanes turned up and joined in the party. The Huns didn't wait for more, but scattered and fled pell-mell, jettisoning their bombs on open country. I had helped to turn away the bombers from London! I yelled and whistled with joy, then pounced on the one I had crippled on my first attack. The Hurricanes were seeing off the others OK, so I left them to it.

He appeared to be having difficulty with one engine; I fixed that by stopping it all together for him. He looked a bit lop-sided then, so I stopped the other one too, and he started a long, steep glide down. I saw the rear gunner bale out, so I went up very close and had a look at the aeroplane. It was pretty well riddled, eight machine guns certainly made a mess! I had a look at the pilot. He sat bolt upright in his seat, and was either dead or wounded, for he didn't even turn his head to look at me or watch out for a place to land, but stared straight ahead.

Suddenly, a pair of legs appeared, dangling from the underneath hatch. The other gunner was baling out. He got as far as his waist, then the legs kicked. They became still for a moment, then wriggled again, they writhed, thrashed and squirmed. Good God, he's stuck! Poor devil, he couldn't get in or out, and his legs, all I could see of them, flailed about wildly as he tried to release himself. It was my fault, I suddenly felt guilty and almost physically sick, until I thought of all the people down below, wives, young mothers, kiddies, huddled together in their shelters, waiting for the All-Clear.

The legs still wriggled and thrashed, 2,000 feet above the cool green fields, trapped in a doomed aircraft, gliding down, a dead pilot at the controls. First one boot came off, then the other. He had no socks on; his feet were quite bare; it was pathetic. He'd better hurry, or it would be too late. He hadn't got out before they were down to 1,000. He'd be cut in half when they hit the ground, like cheese on a grater. In spite of all he stood for, he didn't deserve a death like that. I got my sights squarely on where his body would be, and pressed the button. The legs were still, the machine went on. The pilot was dead, he made no attempt to flatten out and land, but went smack into a field and the aeroplane exploded. I saw pieces sail past me as I flew low overhead. I didn't feel particularly jubilant.'

[*The Dornier crashed just north of Sturry in Kent. Bodie had been posted to 66 Squadron at Duxford in May 1940 and was promoted to flying officer a year later. His record stood at five destroyed, five shared destroyed, one unconfirmed destroyed, eight probables and two shared probables, three damaged and one shared damaged. He was killed in a flying accident on February 24, 1942 aged 21 years, possibly while performing acrobatics.*]

A dead German flyer lies in a field near Tangmere on Battle of Britain Day.

Flying Officer Richard George Barclay, 249 Squadron:

'I lay down and immediately became unconscious as if doped....what seemed the next moment I woke with a terrific start to see everyone pouring out of the hut..... I could hear the telephone orderly repeating: "Dover 26,000; fifty plus bandits approaching from the south-east".

Percy shouted, 'Scramble George, lazy bastard!' and automatically I ran out. Parachute on, pulled into cockpit by crew who had already started the engine. Straps helmet, gloves, check the knobs, taxi out, get into right position in my section and take off. I put the R/T on, and only then do I wake up and realise I am in the air flying No. 2 in yellow section.'

[*On this day Flying Officer Barclay shot down a Dornier do 17, probably destroyed two others and damaged a fourth. His final total was 12 either destroyed or claimed as 'probables' with another two shared and four damaged.*

He was promoted to flight lieutenant on October 3, 1941. In April 1942 he was posted abroad to Egypt to command 238 Squadron in July. On his second sortie on July 17 he was shot down by Lt. Werner Schroer of III/JG 27 and killed. He was 22 years old. He is buried in the El Alamein Cemetery and is commemorated on a plaque in Cromer parish church, where his father was vicar from 1939 - 1946.]

Hans Zonderlind, German 'front gunner' in a Dornier Do 17Z:

'From the time that we had been over Maidstone until reaching the outskirts of London, we had been under extreme pressure. The British fighters had been with us since we first crossed the English coast and had gathered in intensity all the time. Our escort had been doing a grand job with the Spitfires at keeping them away from us, and we thought that should things remain like this, then this bombing run would be made easy.

We saw the Hurricanes coming towards us and it seemed that the whole of the RAF was there - we had never seen so many British fighters coming at us at once. I saw a couple of our comrades go down, and we got hit once but it did no real damage.

All around us were dogfights as the fighters went after each other. Then, as we were getting ready for our approach to the target, we saw what must have been a hundred RAF fighters coming at us. We thought that this must have been all the RAF planes up at once, but where were they coming from? We had been told that the RAF fighters were very close to extinction. We could not keep our present course, so we turned to starboard and did all we could to avoid the fighters. After a while I am sure we had lost our bearings, so we just dropped our bombs and made our retreat.'

Squadron Leader Peter Townsend, 85 Squadron:

'Some of us would die within the next few days. That was inevitable. But you did not believe that it would be you. Death was always present, and we knew it for what it was. If we had to die, we would be alone, smashed to pieces, burnt alive or drowned.

Some strange, protecting veil kept the nightmare thought from our minds, as did the loss of our friends. Their disappearance struck us as less a solid blow than a dark shadow which chilled our hearts and passed on.'

[*Peter Townsend had a very distinguished RAF career and his war tally totalled nine destroyed, two shared, two 'probables' and four damaged. He had several promotions and ended the war as a group captain. He shot down the first enemy aircraft to crash on English soil - a Heinkel He 111 of 4/KG26 which crashed 5 miles south of Whitby on February 3, 1940. (For the first to crash on British soil - in Scotland - see page 9)*

In mid-February 1944 he was appointed equerry to King George VI, and he was romantically linked to Princess Margaret. He retired from the RAF in November 1956, having been made a CVO. He died in 1995.]

Major Adolph Galland III/JG 26:

'Our greatest mistake was not keeping the pressure up on the airfields of southern England. Goering thought that he was master when he said that he was now in charge of the battle. He thought he was losing too many aircraft in attacking the RAF airfields. They were always there, not in great numbers, but they were always there.

He thought that by trying to bomb London by night (he knew that Britain had no night fighter squadrons) he could devastate London and that the people of Britain would be crying for mercy. This was his greatest mistake. He himself gave the RAF room to breathe, time to re-organise, time to rebuild. The result was, we were losing the Battle of Britain.'

Unteroffizier Walburger's Messerschmitt 109 crash-landed near Uckfield after being shot down during the noon action on Battle of Britain Day. His aircraft is seen here some weeks later besided a boarded-up Nelson's Column in Trafalgar Square, where it was placed on exhibition as part of a National Savings drive.

September 27

F riday September 27 started damp and cloudy, with prolonged showers in the London area. The first signs of a build up of enemy aircraft appeared on the operations table around 8am. These aircraft were chiefly bomb-carrying Bf 110s escorted by Bf 109s. They were soon harried by the British fighters and very quickly dropped their bombs indiscriminately before retreating across the Channel.

A few of the Bf 109s made it as far as the London area, initially waiting for another formation of bombers made up of Dornier Do 17s and Junkers Ju 88s. These bombers, however, were intercepted over the coast on their way in by a number of Spitfire and Hurricane squadrons. In the meantime the 109s were attacked, and quickly made a dive for the safety of a ground-level retreat.

The Luftwaffe, having failed to clear the skies of the British fighters, reverted at 11.30am to a split raid, sending 80 aircraft to Bristol: these were mainly from Stab Erprobungs Gruppe 210 and included Junkers Ju 88s and Bf 110s. Another 300 aircraft were sent to London - Junker Ju 88s and Heinkel He 111's mainly from KG 51, 53, 54 and 77. These were escorted by Bf 109s, most of which came from JG27.

No. 10 Group sent their squadrons to fight the Bristol raiders, the combats stretching right across the west country, and, as a result, just a few Bf 109s and Bf 110s managed to get through into a bombing position. These were inter-cepted by the Nottingham Squadron on the outskirts of the city, forcing them to release their bombs on the suburbs.

Meanwhile, the raiders attacking London fared little better, as the majority reached no further than the middle of Kent, where they were so severely mauled that they fled in utter confusion. A few did manage to reach the city and cause some damage with their bombs, but it was classed as a minor raid - London accepting that it was lucky on this occasion.

Records seen after the war indicate it was another bad day for the Luftwaffe, losing 55 aircraft of which about half were bombers. The Channel was alive with air sea rescue planes and boats for most of the late afternoon and evening. Most of the 28 British Fighters that were lost came down on land.

Cyril Babbage, looking out from the hut at the weather that morning remarked that it wasn't a very good day for flying and hoped that they weren't going to be called for a 'scramble' However, that wasn't to be, as a few minutes later the telephone shouted its message - the area, once again, Kent.

Sandy Johnstone, back from a few days leave, was leading 'A' Flight over Dungeness when half a dozen Bf 109s bounced them from a great height. It was rather fortunate for them that Babbage, who was very aware of high flying Bf 109s, saw them in time and gave the warning. There was time enough for the

Spitfires to 'side-step', allowing the German fighters to pass harmlessly by. Babbage, on the outside of the flight, managed to draw a bead on one of the 109s, but to no avail. It was fairly obvious that they didn't want to mix it with the British fighters, maintaining their speed as they went out of sight.

> 'On the morning of September 27 I was returning from a sortie in the Dover area when I spied a Heinkel 111 north of Brighton being attacked at low level by a pair of Hurricanes. One engine was smoking badly, and a member of the crew had baled out.
>
> As several pilots of 602 were by now highly decorated, I decided that this was the moment to distinguish myself. Pumping all my remaining ammunition into the crippled Heinkel, I hurried back to Westhampnett and was delighted to inform our intelligence officer Henry Graysbrook that I had definitely broken the ice, and that the evidence was in a field.
>
> I don't think the Hurricane pilots got my aircraft number, otherwise they might have had their revenge at a later date for my kill.'
>
> **Paddy Barthropp**

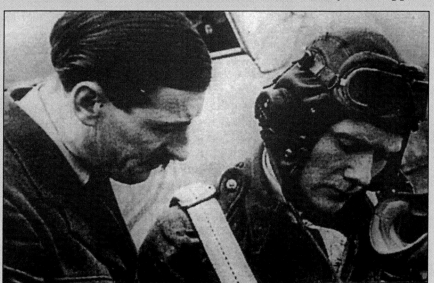

Paddy Barthropp *(left)* had an eventful war. He flew with 602 throughout the Battle of Britain, was shot down over France and was a prisoner of war in the notorious Stalag Luft 3, which featured in the film *The Great Escape*. Barthropp was himself preparing to enter the escape tunnel when the German guards discovered it.

It was now time for 602 to return to base. Within about half an hour the Spitfires were once again ready for action, having been re-fuelled and re-armed, and soon afterwards they were again scrambled. Findlay Boyd led off towards London hoping for some success against the German bombers. The location area for 602 was north Sussex and Kent: a large force of enemy bombers had been mapped heading for the Kent coast.

A number of other squadrons had also been scrambled, including No. 1 (RCAF) Squadron and 72, 73, 92, 213, 303 and 501 Squadrons. The Spitfires and Hurricanes found themselves in a good position to attack as the enemy bombers reached landfall.

Soon the skies were a maelstrom of twisting, turning and diving aircraft, the British fighters reaching to the bottom of their socks in a superhuman effort to repel the invader. First one, then another Bf 109, smoke trailing, was heading for the ground. One parachute was seen drifting lazily earthwards.

About 9.20am, the Spitfire flown by Douglas Gage was attacked by a Bf 109 and sustained damage in the glycol tank. Gage indicated his intention and landed at Birelham Forge Farm, Mayfield, unhurt.

At this stage Babbage was having his own personal war. He selected one of the Junkers Ju 8s and, closing at speed, fired three two-second bursts. Smoke and flames billowed from the doomed bomber as it keeled over towards its port side and went down in an exaggerated arc, levelling out before it crashed in the Kent countryside. His next target was a Bf 109, and he just had time to fire a quick burst before the plane disappeared into cloud.

The newcomer pilot officer Paddy Barthropp, a little bit overwhelmed at what was taking place, soon settled down to the cold fact of attacking the German raiders. He and two Hurricane pilots attacked a Heinkel He 111. 'This one isn't going home,' he thought, and he found himself truly excited as the massive bomber started its death dive. It was a half share, but he had got his first victim and was no longer a virgin fighter. Following this little escapade, John Willie Hopkin, recently transferred in from 54 Squadron, got another.

Although a large number of German aircraft were shot down or damaged, almost every Squadron taking part lost aircraft.

No. 1 Squadron (RCAF), based at Northolt, had three aircraft shot down, losing one pilot. 72 squadron also lost three aircraft, with two pilots killed. 92 squadron from Biggin Hill lost four Spitfires, with two pilots killed. Another of its pilots, Pilot officer Wade, attacked a Dornier Do 17 over Brighton but was hit by return fire. He crash-landed at Lewes race course at speed and overturned, but although badly shaken, he was unhurt.

There were a number of combat areas covering almost the whole of East Sussex and the western half of Kent. 303 Squadron lost five aircraft with two of their pilots killed, the combats taking place over Hailsham. 249 Squadron from North Weald, were mainly involved over northern Sussex, losing one of their Hurricanes, force-landing at Gatwick. Another, involved in a deadly game of cat and mouse, finished by colliding with a Bf 110 during combat over Redhill and crashed in a field at Hailsham, Flying Officer Percy Burton losing his life: a road in the town is named after him.

No losses were inflicted on 602 and, on landing, the men were full of what had happened. Findlay Boyd, the 'B' Flight Commander spoke, in an excited voice to his mechanic: 'It was great, Smithy. You couldn't see the Channel for dead bodies!'

'I don't think he likes Germans,' Smith remarked with a shrug as Findlay cheerfully wandered off. He then got on with the job of cleaning up Boyd's cockpit. The filter cap on the oil tank had come off somehow, making a terrible mess in the cockpit. He poured in a can of petrol and had to wash down the whole of the fuselage. This Spitfire wouldn't be going anywhere for the next few days.

September 30

Monday September 30 witnessed the final major daylight battle. The weather was fair with scattered light cloud - good combat weather. At about 10.30am, 15 Junkers Ju 88 bombers took off from Orleans and Bricey airfields, and one of the crew in particular, Oberst. Helmut Schwenhart, was feeling pretty happy and confident about the job ahead. His aircraft was one of the new Junkers Ju 88A-55s, fitted with better armour and with an increased wingspan. He was 20 years old and this was his 26th mission.

The German formation crossed the Channel at 12,000 feet. He habitually wore an orange scarf in flight as a lucky charm. When his colleagues, asked him about it he would refuse to answer, but in fact it was a present from his mother and he thought it nobody else's business.

The target today was Weymouth. The area itself was nothing to worry about, but the problem was having to fly close to the Isle of Wight. He knew this area was closely guarded and that there were several airfields close by. He hadn't forgotten the last time he was in the vicinity: his flight had been given a very hard time by the Spitfire pilots and he thought himself lucky still to be alive. He didn't fancy another such encounter.

During their briefing, prior to take off, they had been told that London would also be a target, and this would draw the Spitfires to the capital, leaving them clear to bomb. He sank back in his seat, completely relaxed with that thought filling his mind.

The aircraft had left France behind and were now over the English Channel, heading towards the Isle of Wight. Schwenhart told himself that everything would be all right, but deep down there was a little niggle: something was saying 'be careful'.

At Westhampnett, the pilots had been relaxing, having already been up on an entirely fruitless mission. More than a couple of them were dozing in the old arm chairs, but they sat bolt upright when the telephone rang - it had become second nature now. Paddy Barthrupp answered the phone and bellowed in his Irish brogue: 'Scramble, Needles, Angels one five.' He pressed the alarm bell and he was off, quickly covering the area between the hut and his Spitfire.

In no time at all the 11 Spitfire engines were singing, but only ten managed to take off: one engine gave up the ghost before it had travelled more than a few yards. Those that did take off were soon airborne and lined up behind Sandy Johnstone their leader on course for the Isle of Wight.

The pilots of 602 and the German pilots saw each other at about the same time. This was what Helmut Schwenhart had been dreading. Maybe that 'niggle' had been a warning. The Junkers scattered, diving and twisting as best they could, trying to dodge the Spitfires. They knew they were no match for the

Spitfires. The air was filled with lead. With Sandy in the lead, 602 went down into the attack. Two of the Junkers stayed together, possibly thinking they had more chance. Sandy selected these two, getting closer all the time. When there were just a hundred yards between them he pulled out a little to port side, finger on the button, and his bullets tore along the side of the first plane. It blew up and went down straight away, minus part of its wing, performing a series of rolls. The second Junkers was desperately trying to escape. The aircraft had already turned and was heading back across the Channel. Sandy let fly again, hitting it. Losing height, and with smoke trailing from one of the engines, it was allowed to go on its way. 'He won't make it across,' Sandy said to himself.

Above him, the other pilots were having a field day, Pedro Hanbury fired at one of the Junkers and watched, fascinated, as both propellers began to 'windmill'. The aircraft then seemed to come to a complete standstill. The nose went down and in seconds it was in a dive, both engines billowing smoke and flames. No crew members got out, and with an almighty splash the aircraft hit the sea and disappeared.

Pat Lyall, was taking his time, taking pot shots at everything that moved, and he hit a number of the German aircraft. One of them suddenly spurted smoke and flames from one of its engines, the crew leaping out for their lives, while another lost its rudder.

One of the Junkers, badly damaged, just about made it across the Channel, the engines red hot and streaming smoke and flames. It put down into the nearest field, but as it was going in to crash-land part of its tail assembly broke away. The crew managed to get out with nothing more than a few cuts and bruises.

High above the Isle of Wight the Spitfires were enjoying great success, the German pilots in complete confusion. Ginger Whall and Andy McDowall appeared to be in competition with each other. They took care of another two bombers between them, and Whall later readily agreed that his colleague should have the larger share.

Very soon the skies cleared and Sandy Johnstone gave the order to return to base. 'We tangled with twelve unescorted Junkers Ju 88's over the Isle of Wight,' he reported. 'We quickly accounted for six before the rest fled for cover in the clouds. I was firing "sure hit" bullets today and my victim went down minus its port main plane, the engine having exploded dramatically. I saw one Jerry jump out as the Junkers disappeared below me in a series of flat rolls.'

The following simple words were written in the operations book that night: 'A good days work'

Then came an unexpected twist to the story. Sandy Johnstone had a longstanding invitation to dinner on this evening at Arundel Castle, the home of the Duke of Norfolk, and he had been looking forward to it for quite a while. He had had his best 'blues' especially cleaned and pressed and took very special care in his dressing. He had just about finished when Group Captain Jack Boret, the C.O. of Tangmere, called on the telephone. The gist of his message was that

Sandy should call at Tangmere airfield and see Boret on his way to Arundel. This he did, although it meant that he eventually arrived at the castle full of apologies for being late. He had, however, a strange story to tell his hosts.

When Sandy had shot down the Junkers Ju 88 over Bembridge, Isle of Wight, he had noticed that one of the crew had baled out, but he thought no more about it. This German had, in fact, landed safely and had been captured. Taken to Tangmere airfield and placed in the guardroom, he insisted on meeting the Spitfire pilot who had shot him down.

Jack Boret introduced Sandy to the German, who clicked his heels in salute, forced a rather embarrassed smile and then, explaining that he wouldn't be needing them any more, presented 602's commanding officer with his Luger pistol, his flying helmet, his lifejacket and, lastly, an orange scarf. Sandy saluted and accepted the gifts. Oberst. Helmut Schwenhart had managed to bale out in the nick of time.

From the horse's mouth . . .

'When we were up in Scotland we used to get most of our information from the barmaid at the local pub. She was better informed than any of us. One night she said she'd heard rumours that our squadron was moving south. When I rang Group that night they said: "Oh yes, we were going to tell you. You're going south the day after tomorrow." We were pleased to be heading into the heavy combat area. We had heard that the squadrons down there were knocking up big scores on enemy aircraft. That was the great thing, and we wanted to get in on it.'

Squadron Leader Sandy Johnstone

'We were losing planes every day but heard terrible things about replacements for them. We heard that certain maintenance units where Hurricanes were being assembled to come to us were closed on Saturdays and Sundays. Beaverbrook stopped all that. He said: "Twenty-four hours a day solid working, seven days a week." That was Beaver. He petrified people into working, and the aeroplanes started coming to us.'

Pilot Officer Dennis David

'A few brave buggers used to do head-on attacks. Bloody dangerous. There were one or two lunatics who revelled in it. The chance of hitting something going head-on was pretty remote unless you were attacking a big formation of bombers. Then you would rake them, getting your nose up and down, knowing something was going to connect. That was very effective.'

Pilot Officer Paddy Barthropp

'Within two hours [of a forced landing] I was up flying again. You didn't have any shock - it didn't seem to worry you. It would now. I mean, if I miss another car by an inch it takes me about a week to recover. It was unlike the Navy or the Army: you didn't really see anyone killed. If you saw somebody shot at, you only saw an aircraft and you just hoped the bugger would bale out. If he crash-landed somewhere, you never saw it.

Pilot Officer Glen 'Nuts' Niven

Battle of Britain – Phase 5

October 1 – October 31

*T*hree months less ten days had now elapsed since the start of the Battle of Britain, but for all the German's effort of attacking airfields and, later, of bombing towns and cities, little had been gained. They had failed to destroy the RAF, had lost more than 1600 aircraft and, as a result. were unable to invade Britain.

In an effort to avoid further bomber losses the Luftwaffe resorted to the use of fighter-bombers operating at high altitude. This lessened the accuracy of the bombings, but the aircraft were safer from British attack. Not only were the

Spitfires on patrol, October/November 1940. 'Nuts' Niven describes this type of patrol flying on p. 115.

bombers difficult to track and counter at a greater height, but the Bf 109 fighter with its two-stage supercharger had a superior performance over the Hurricane and Spitfire above 25,000 feet. The other problem for the RAF was that its pilots had no idea which of the incoming enemy aircraft were carrying bombs and should therefore be selected for attack.

A tactic developed to try to minimise these problems was employed at the end of September. A new flight was formed - 421 Flight (later Number 91 Squadron) - to spot approaching enemy formations and report their height and strength to the controllers at Uxbridge. The pilots' orders were to fly high and avoid any combats. During the first ten days of October four of these aircraft had been shot down, and they were therefore ordered to fly in pairs. This was, however, still an insufficient response to the problem of the high-flying raiders.

It was about this time that six Blenheims and two Defiant squadrons were made available for night fighting, assisted by a flight of Hurricanes. They were gradually fitted with air interception radar (AIR), an innovation at that time. However, the number of night interceptions remained disappointing, with just a few enemy aircraft shot down.

Not until 1941 would the night fighter squadrons begin to have a telling effect on the Luftwaffe. In the meantime some of the more experienced Hurricane and Spitfire pilots attempted to convert themselves to night fighting without being properly trained for the job or having the basic essentials for approach and landing at their home airfields.

The courageous risks our pilots took in appalling weather were rewarded with little success, even on bright moonlit nights. The Luftwaffe had little opposition during their night bombing raids, although there is some evidence to show that the flak put up by the anti-aircraft guns did force the bombers to fly at a higher altitude and encourage the more half-hearted German crews to turn back. Certainly the sound of the firing guns was comforting for civilians, who believed that they were blasting German bombers from the night skies.

October 1

The Luftwaffe decided on three main targets for the first day of October - London again, of course, together with Southampton and Portsmouth. The first sign of any raiders was about 7am when they were spotted in the Beachy Head area. They were flying high and soon moved away.

The first main attack came from aircraft based in the Caen area of France. They were plotted at 10.45am as they crossed the Channel heading for Southampton and Portsmouth. The difference on this raid was that the aircraft consisted of Bf 110s and Bf 109s only. Some of these were the bomb carriers. It was the first real indication that the German bombers had been soundly beaten on the daylight attacks and were now concentrating night raids on selected targets, with London being in the forefront. It was now pretty certain that the fighter arm of the Luftwaffe would have to be responsible for both the bombing and the fighting.

Approximately a third of the German fighters, some 250 aircraft, were about to be converted to carrying bombs, a new experience for the fighter pilots. The Bf 109s were to carry a single 250kg. bomb while the Bf 110s would carry a total bomb-load of 700kg.

Flying at great heights and taking every advantage of cloudy weather, these aircraft gave Fighter Command yet another problem - the many fruitless hours of climb and chase. Little else occurred, however, and so Fighter Command continued the great recovery which it had started on September 7.

At Westhampnett it was to be a rather special day. Sandy had invited the Duke of Norfolk to visit the station and meet his men. Fingers were kept tightly crossed that the Luftwaffe wouldn't call and spoil the occasion. The pilots were dressed ready for action as the Duke arrived, and one might have thought that the Luftwaffe were listening in: within minutes the telephone rang, a voice shouted 'Scramble' and that was the end of that.

Through the R/T sandy instructed his squadron to make for the Isle of Wight at Angels one five, and they got there in double quick time. The area was covered by thick cloud, although broken in places. The pilots knew that this could be very dangerous for them. The German aircraft were about - but where?

A fair sized force of 109s suddenly pounced on them from behind a bank of cumulus cloud. It was fortunate that Paddy Barthropp saw them and gave a warning, since it allowed the squadron time to dodge out of the way. On this sortie 602 were flying with no fewer than four new pilots, and once again they were heavily outnumbered. One of the new pilots, John Willie Hopkin, was the first to fire at a 109 as it whizzed past , and although he didn't score, it suggested to his commanding officer that he perhaps had no need to worry overmuch about his new recruits. As it happened, Hopkin was the only one to let fire, as the German fighters, covering their tracks with the clouds, were not seen again.

When this was reported back to Tangmere, the controller insistied that the enemy aircraft were still showing on his plot. He eventually sent 602 to investigate a report of firing in the area of the Needles. That area having been patrolled without success, the order was given to return to base.

Back at Westhampnett, the pilots were pleased to discover that the Duke of Norfolk was still there, just finishing his third cup of coffee. After all, he had come to meet the lads and that was what he was going to do. There were no more calls to action, and the visit extended throughout the day, the bar in the officers' mess being well and truly used.

It appears that 602 had been sent up to assist 607 Squadron from Tangmere, which had lost two Hurricanes over the Isle of Wight, with both pilots killed. Another squadron, 238 from Chilbolton, had also been involved, losing two Hurricanes: one of the pilots baled out, while the other was posted as missing, possibly lost, over Poole Harbour.

October 7

*A*ir Vice-Marshal Keith Park visited the base on Moday October 7. A tall New Zealander, he was responsible for 602 and the other squadrons within 11 Group, and for this first visit the place had been subject to a little 'spit and polish'. He arrived on time , flying his own Hurricane.

Never mind the visiting New Zealander: the Squadron was now getting a

Air Vice-Marshal Keith Park, commander of 11 Group.

Canadian feel about it. This was particularly noticeable over the R/T. Jake Edy had been with the squadron for a while and was gradually inching his way towards getting a DFC. He had been joined by Pilot Officer Johnny Hart, and when 'Nuts' Niven was posted back to the squadron that made three. Sandy joked that things were getting serious: Scottish accentswere being replaced by Canadian ones.

Park congratulated the Westhampnett crews on doing an excellent job, and the pilots seemed to sense that he would soon see for himself just what they were capable of - one or two in particular seemed to be acting like cats on a hot tin roof, unable to relax.

Their premonition was justified. Soon after lunch had been taken, the telephone bell sounded. Eleven Spitfires took to the skies, the first group with Sandy Johnstone including Donald Jack and Pedro Hanbury, with Ginger Whall just behind.

The squadron had now settled into their formation, closed down their canopies and were making occasional glances across at each other, accompanied by the usual clenched fist or V-for-Victory sign. Meanwhile 607 and 213 Squadrons were also scrambled, twelve Hurricanes from each Squadron, the idea being to rendezvous together and proceed to the target. Jimmie Vick was leading 607 and Stu MacDonald 213.

Just before reaching Worthing, two Hurricanes of 607 Squadron acting as 'tail end Charlies' came close together, moved away and closed in again. The Spitfire pilots, flying at a higher altitude, and could see clearly what was happening. Every moment they expected the two Hurricanes to move away from each other but, as if drawn by a magnet, they kept on the same deadly course and collided in mid-air. The two aircraft seemed for a brief second to be holding each other in some sort of embrace. Then they both went down, the aircraft crashing near Slindon. Pilot Officer Scott baled out, safely landing without injury, but Flying Officer Difford, the other pilot, was killed.

Donald Jack wondered if this was some sort of omen: what a start to a sortie, and the enemy hadn't even been spotted yet! This was an unaccustomed thought, as he wasn't the superstitious type, and he quickly dismissed it from his mind. Pilots had lost their lives for suffering a lapse in concentration.

The plotters had tracked the enemy aircraft to a point offshore, but they were still flying westwards. The three squadrons were ordered to change course and head towards Portland. Proceeding west, they soon arrived over Weymouth, but still they saw nothing. This was strange, as in the past they would have spotted vast formations of German aircraft and now there wasn't a single one in sight. They were approaching the outskirts of 10 Group territory.

Further orders came through: they were to return to the Southampton area while the squadrons of 10 Group would take over from them. With all eyes peeled, still they saw no enemy aircraft. The Germans , they thought, must have turned tail or flown much further west. In fact the target was the Westland Aircraft factory at Yeovil.

Johnstone gave the order to return to base, and they wheeled round ready to go home. Just then, however, information came through that a solitary, unidentified aircraft had appeared near Brighton: 'Villa Leader, we have a bogey at Angels ten over Brighton; can we have a section on it, please?' 'Villa Blue One [Donald Jack] from Villa Leader; Go on Donald, have a go will you, yes?'

Jack, together with his number 2, Ginger Whall, broke from the formation and headed eastwards, following the coastline, while the remainder of the squadron headed for Westhampnett. The two Spitfires neared Brighton, their pilots' pulses racing, their eyes searching for the interloper.

It could of course be 'one of ours', so that great care was needed. At just on 5.45pm, close to a cloud, an aircraft was spotted, only to disappear into cloud. A few more hundred feet, and then out it came - not one of ours, but a Dornier Do 17. The pilot was totally unaware of the Spitfires. Donald Jack first spotted the 'bogey' saying: 'Blue Two, bandit, see him just below us, Tally Ho!'

First Jack, accelerating, pounced on the German bomber, his bullets hitting the wing root and starboard engine. He had closed to within about 70 feet before pulling away and climbing upwards. Now Whall - flying Findlay Boyd's Spitfire today - had his turn, making an accurate pass over the bomber and raking it with fire. His bullets struck the centre section and cabin area.

Jack made a complete circle and watched as the bomber straightened out for a brief second or so and then plunged into the waters of the English Channel. No parachutes were seen to come from the aircraft.

'Good shooting, Blue Two, let's go home,' Jack called.

Whall closed up, level on Jack's starboard side, and the two Spitfires wheeled around and started for home. Suddenly, however, and without any warning,

Jack saw the other plane peeling away from him and losing height.

'Villa Blue Two, what's up; have you a problem?'

There was no reply. Again Jack called: still nothing. By this timeWhall had lost a lot of height and was still going down. Jack followed, screaming at the top of his voice: 'Get out, for God's sake, get out, get out, get out!' But nothing - no word from Ginger.

The Spitfire crashed near Courts Farm at Lullington. Ginger Whall, severely injured, was taken to the Princess Alice Hospital at Eastbourne, where he died shortly after admission.

Donald Jack rather shakily returned to Westhampnett on his own. The others suspected something was wrong when Ginger's Spitfire failed to return with him. Visibly upset, Jack attempted to explain what had happened, although he would never be able to understand it.

Ginger Whall, who was killed this day. Was his Spitfire sabotaged?

There had been no return fire from the Dornier. Pilot blackout was a possibility, but sabotage was always suspected when unexplained crashes occurred. Terrible to contemplate, but could that be the explanation?

Jack spent the evening in the mess with the other officers, but he really wasn't in the mood. He would never claim it was one of his better days, and he retired early, sleep probably being his salvation.

● On this day Fighter Command flew 825 sorties and lost 17 aircraft to the Luftwaffe's 21, one of which was an He 115 seaplane.

Examination of eight Bf 109s shot down revealed that they were from LG 2 and that each carried a 250kg bomb. They were operating in small formations of between 6 and 18 aircraft, and were flying two or three sorties a day.

Far from being progressively weakened, the RAF was fighting back with increased strength.

Goering's new plan . . .

In Berlin Goering now put forward a new five point plan for the war against Britain. He frankly admitted that the demoralisation of London and the Provinces was one of his aims, and he described the air offensive as 'merely an initial phase'.

The plan he outlined was:

1 Absolute control of the Channel and the English coastal areas.

2 Progressive and complete annihilation of London, with all its military installations and industrial production.

3. A steady paralysing of Britain's technical, commercial, industrial and civil life.

4. Demoralisation of the civilian population of London and its provinces.

5. The progressive weakening of Britain's armed forces.

'Nuts' Niven Remembers . . .

'The tactics in 1940 were that 12 aircraft, Spitfires as far as we were concerned, would take off, three in a 'V' formation, three in a 'V' formation behind them and a further three behind them. One other plane, then the final two who would act as 'weavers.' One would fly above and behind and the other below and behind. These two 'weavers' were there to keep a lookout backwards in case the formation was attacked from behind. So I was the boy at the back weaving, spending my time trying not to lose the squadron.

When the C.O. sighted the enemy he would order 'Line astern'. This meant that the C.O. would be at the front, his number two would come back and underneath him, and the number three would come back and go under number two. The next three had to go in behind these and so on. This way you would find the squadron stretched out for two or three miles. I would be at the back, usually hanging about doing around 120 mph. By the time the rest were in combat attacking the German aircraft I was about five miles behind and saying, 'Wait for me, please!'

Being Spitfires, we were nearly always higher up. To give you some idea, I never saw a bomber the entire Battle of Britain, and it was mostly Messerschmitt 109s we dealt with.

Glen Niven's logbook for late October, 1940.

I wasn't actually hit or clobbered until October, and again I was right at the back. Their leader was coming down and attacking me in the bum – which I didn't like very much. That's why I think it was a ridiculous formation to fly and, in fact, the next year we followed the German fashion of 'figure-of-fours': that was three lots of four, so that you weren't behind but alongside everybody and everyone could get into the action right away. With the old way, the first three or four of the line astern pilots were usually the only ones who could see the enemy and fire at them. The rest of us were charging along trying to catch up.

I think we would have shot more down with the figure of fours, because more pilots would have had the chance to be at the front. To be honest - let's face it - about 10 per cent of the pilots shot down about 80 per cent of the enemy planes. The other 90 per cent of the pilots were charging about, usually being too late to join in with the main action, and that meant that they continued to be pretty inexperienced.

The action in October was the first time I had fired my guns. Previous to that I had been keeping out of the way. Once again I was at the back of things when we were attacking the Messerschmitt 109s. One of them flew absolutely straight at me and fired head on. I recall saying, ' Bugger this for a lark' and squirting a few at him. We both missed by a country mile I suppose, and when he whipped by me I saw it was a Spitfire! I mean, the number of Spitfires who fired at Spitfires - Christ, I didn't need this! When he came at me it was just two wings and a blob. He fired first - I'll give him that - and I squirted back, and off he went. While we were looking at each other and saying, 'Oh well, thank God we missed' what

The damaged wing of Glen 'Nuts' Nivens Spitfire. He landed safely.

was definitely a 109 got on my backside, because I looked just to the left and there were tracer bullets about a foot away from the cockpit. That was unhealthy. I thought: 'This is it, this is where Niven dies, something drastic and quick!'

So, the great thing was, 'Bottom left, top right', which meant ('bottom left') you put on full left rudder, which was towards the aileron, because that made you skid away from them, and ('top right') with your stick you turned the aircraft upside down and the wrong way around. So the chances of the enemy following you were almost nil.

As I backed up - this is why I knew it was a 109 - a cannon shell hit me and blew my wing tip apart. There was one hell of a bang. It sounded as if a sledge-hammer had hit it. The force was tremendous, so much so that it threw me upside down and once again I thought, 'This is it, what a bright way to go!'

I pulled the stick right back and went down twisting and turning in all directions and heading down towards the ground, the speed increasing. We were about 25,000 feet when this happened, and I said, 'Our Father which art in Heaven, get this sod off my tail.' I continued to drop, and at 5,000 feet and getting the thing up to about 350mph I pulled out very gently with all things crossed, hoping the aircraft would stay in one piece. It had just been severely tested, as I had. Luckily the 109 hadn't followed me all the way down, but my wing tip was flapping away and I knew I had been extremely lucky in getting away with my life. However, I was still a long way from home - all this had happened over the Kent countryside.

I now set about finding my way back to base. We did have maps but you soon knew your way around the south of England and could find Westhampnett quite easily. Railways and the coastline were the main help. You came down low to see where the hell you were. I tottered slowly along, on my own, as the others had long gone. I was the last to arrive, and it was all very dramatic because I had been up for close on two hours and everybody was waiting for me to appear.

I landed with the wing tip falling off, and just then the engine stopped as the fuel ran out. The Spitfire would glide very far and so you looked for a decent field and landed, 90 per cent of the time with your wheels UP. If you put them down there was a bloody good chance of up-ending the aircraft and being stuck underneath with two large petrol tanks in your lap.

There was an amusing conclusion to this flight, as I was the last to land on our rather small field and, seeing that my plane had been damaged, the medical officer leapt aboard the ambulance saying, 'Follow that aircraft'. Unfortunately the ambulance driver put the vehicle in reverse and went straight backwards into the hedge.

October 12

Saturday, October 12 was a bad day, with the strain telling. The squadron was scrambled, together with the Hurricanes of 145 from Tangmere and 257 from North Weald and the Biggin Hill Spitfires of 72 and 92 squadrons.They were vectored towards south east Kent to deal with a number of enemy aircraft which had been plotted gathering in the Calais area. The British pilots were ready as the enemy aircraft reached the coast. The Hurricanes were soon in action, quickly followed by the others.

The attacking enemy aircraft consisted mainly of bomb-carrying 109s with a group of others acting as escorts. The Spitfires and Hurricanes were involved in numerous dog-fights stretching from Hastings to Dungeness and many miles northwards. As the battle raged, aircraft of both sides were being shot down, with pilots baling out of their burning and crashing machines. A Hurricane of 145 Squadron was shot down over Hastings, the wounded pilot baling out and coming down safely at Guestling. He was taken to the Buchanan Hospital in Hastings. Another crashed near Cranbrook, the pilot losing his life, while a third, badly damaged, just made it back to base. A Spitfire of 72 Squadron lost formation and crashed near Folkestone.

A Bf 109E-4 of Stab II/JG54 was involved in a deadly duel with a Spitfire of 92 Squadron flown by the 24-year-old Fl/Lt. Robert Stanford Tuck, who had already accounted for 14 confirmed 'kills' and was about to get his 15th. The Bf 109 came around in a wide arc, which was just what Tuck had hoped for: a short burst and the German raider was on the way down, force-landing near Tenterden. Its pilot, Lt. Malischewski, was captured. (Tuck, a wing commander by the end of the war, was shot down over France in January 1942 and became a prisoner of war. By that time he had become one of Britain's top Aces with 27 enemy aircraft destroyed, six probables and another six damaged.)

Several other Bf 109s were either shot down or made their way back across the Channel suffering some sort of damage.

602 returned to base, but soon after 3pm the bell at dispersal signalled the 'Scramble' for a similar mission. Among those taking off were Cyril Babbage and John Hart. Messerschmitts from JG 52 were soon in combat, and the British pilots managed to get the better of them, three of them being shot down in quick succession. All three pilots baled out, two of them wounded and coming down in the Ashford area. Two others were shot down and crashed into the sea, while another two crash-landed in France.

On this occasion several Junkers Ju 88s were with the Bf 109s, and one of them made a dash from the scene towards Eastbourne. Hart and Babbage were soon after it, determined that it wasn't going to make it home. The two Spitfires went in for the kill, but the German gunners on board were giving a very good account of themselves, determined to fight to the finish. Both Spitfire pilots struck home, causing damage to the German bomber, but it wouldn't go down and was eventually to limp home across the Channel. In their turn the German gunners must have been in top form, as they hit both the incoming two Spitfires. By this time the action had moved out over the sea off Beachy Head. Hart's aircraft suffered damage to the main spar, but he managed to nurse it home to Westhampnett, where it was later repaired.

Meanwhile Babbage's Spitfire had suffered damage to the glycol system. Not fancying another early bath, he coaxed his aircraft back towards land, losing height all the time.He knew that there were plenty of grassy fields to the north of Newhaven. He hoped to come in over the town and land close to one of the farms, and as landfall approached he selected a field and dropped his wheels. He knew his speed was a little to fast and, although he landed safely, he ploughed through some hedges and overturned, finishing in a 'wheels up' position at Iford, about half way between Newhaven and Lewes. He scrambled out and, apart from a slight cut and a bruise or two, was unhurt. Before being taken back to base he enjoyed some refreshment at the farmhouse, to the great excitement of the farmer's children.

At Westhampnett there were great celebrations in the sergeants' mess when it was discovered that Babbage's award of a DFM had been confirmed. It was also announced that Findlay Boyd had been awarded a second DFC. The squadron's gongs were steadily mounting.

• The point had now been reached at which Hitler had to decide on his next course of action. It was evident towards the end of September that the invasion of Britain could not be undertaken before the winter. Bomber Command had already sunk more than 200 of the German barges which were to be used for the invasion.

The following letter was circulated to the German High Command:

'The Fuhrer has decided that from now until the spring, preparations for 'Sealion' shall be continued solely for the purpose of maintaining political and military pressure on England.

Should the invasion be reconsidered in the spring or early summer of 1941, orders for a renewal of operational readiness will be issued later. In the meantime military conditions for a later invasion are to be improved.'

The significance of this memorandum was not to be realised at the War Office (which had been damaged by a bomb at 9pm on this day) until very much later. Hitler had in effect admitted defeat nineteen days before the Battle of Britain officially came to a close.

The Final Chapter

November – December 1940

The squadron had now been in the forefront of the battle for twelve weeks and the pilots were very weary from the sustained combats and sorties that had been played out over the southern counties - many of them taking place over the beautiful Sussex countryside.

For all this, the early days of November saw the squadron record some of its best results, and there were several acts of derring-do to recount back at base after successful jousts with German fighters.

During a number of sorties and skirmishes over the southern counties, for instance, John Willie Hopkin suddenly found himself in the midst of a group of Messerschmitt 109s over the Isle of Wight. One of the German pilots had him in his sights, but Hopkin managed to get inside of him and then the tables were turned. The Bf 109 slipped him and made off across the Channel but not before he had been hit, the tell-tale smoke streaming behind as the aircraft began to drift lower and lower. Although it was later lost from view, this would certainly count as a 'probable'.

One pilot who had been in the thick of it from the beginning was Pat Lyall. On November 6, with another raid on Southampton seemingly imminent, 602 and 145 Squadrons engaged Messerschmitts from Major Helmut Wick's JG 2 'Richthofen' Geschwader between Shoreham and the Isle of Wight. Andy McDowall claimed two Bf 109s destroyed, and succeeded in shooting down the Messerschmitt flown by Oberfeldwebel Heinrick Klopp, who baled out near Ventnor, Isle of Wight. German ships were sent out to the area to look for him but he wasn't found. McDowall claimed another Bf 109 destroyed, sharing it with a Hurricane of 145 Squadron, while Hopkin and Lyall joined forces to attack two Bf 109s, claiming them both as 'shared probables'.

Once again 602 Squadron sustained no casualties, but 145 Squadron was not so lucky, losing two Hurricanes. Both pilots baled out, but one got out too low and was killed.

On November 5 a scramble at lunchtime saw Sandy Johnstone and Nigel Rose come face to face with a Junkers Ju 88 which emerged from clouds over Bognor. It was difficult to say who was more surprised. The German pilot pulled away sharply in an effort to return to the clouds and safety, but the bomber gave a broadside view to the two Spitfire pilots who took full advantage.

Sandy later said: 'I saw bullets ripping into the pale blue underside, and when the aircraft swung upright the rear gun was pointing vertically upwards and the gunner was slumped over his scarf ring. Unfortunately, it then dived into a cloud and we lost him.' The intelligence officer allowed their claim for a 'damaged'.

Soon after 5pm the following day two Spitfires flown by Dunlop Urie and Nigel Rose were sent to intercept a lone German bomber on the West Sussex / Hampshire border. This aircraft, a Junkers Ju 88 ,was soon spotted and attacked over Tangmere. Bullets were seen to hit the enemy aircraft, but it somehow stayed in the air and was able to crash-land in France.

On November 13 an improvement in the weather encouraged a number of single German bombers to fly into British air space. There were a number of small clashes with Bf 109s, mainly over Kent. The first main combat took place late in the morning, when three 602 Spitfires patrolling over Brighton, and piloted by Dunlop Urie, Findlay Boyd and John Hart, engaged a Junkers Ju 88 to the north of the town. They were supported by two pilots from 145 Squadron, based at Tangmere, who had just arrived on the scene. The German bomber made a desperate attempt to escape, the pilot using all his guile and cunning, but the British pilots chased it out to sea and shot it down about 15 miles off the Sussex coast. The Junkers landed tail first in the sea with no survivors. All five British pilots were awarded joint credit for the bomber's destruction.

The afternoon was to develop into a 'cat and mouse' game as 602 and a number of other squadrons were vectored to an area that included the Isle of Wight as lone raiders were stalked and chased through the clouds. One or two of them were believed damaged, with members of their crews wounded and in some cases killed. These aircraft however managed to make their way back across the Channel: there were no reports of any German bombers crashing on British soil.

Two days later Westhampnett was struck by a sudden outbreak of flu that floored a number of the pilots, necessitating the recall of those who were enjoying a spot of well-earned leave. Sandy led the squadron during the mid morning as Messerschmitt Bf 109s were tracked at just about every location along the south coast. They returned without having spotted any enemy aircraft.

Around mid afternoon, after another false alarm, the 602 pilots were on patrol over the Spithead area. A couple of Bf 109s were seen at a height of about 27,000 feet, and the Spitfire, having been frustrated on two occasions earlier in the day, were determined to go for them. They climbed steadily to 25,000 feet and were about to launch their attack when other Bf 109s from JG 2 came out of the sun, diving down at speed.

The British pilots were in trouble. The sky was soon full of tracer and bullets, and it seemed close to a miracle that the whole squadron wasn't wiped out. In the event, Andy McDowall was the only one to get hit. He force-landed at Birdham, near Chichester, with shrapnel wounds to his face - a fact which did nothing to improve his looks, temper or language. Uffz. Rudolf Miese was shot down in the incident but he managed to bale out and was captured, his aircraft crashing offshore at Felpham.

By November 18 the list of sick and injured at Westhampnett was growing; Andy McDowall was off, being treated for the wounds to his face, while Cyril Babbage had succumbed to the flu bug. Three new pilots who were due to be posted to the squadron for some unknown reason failed to turn up. The whole squadron listened intently to the wireless in the mess as Prime Minister Winston Churchill told the nation that the pilots of Fighter Command had saved them from a German invasion.

As the year-end drew nearer, attacks by the Luftwaffe grew fewer and fewer. The aircraft that did cross the Channel were mainly photo reconnaissance planes or raiders over the southern counties using the cloud as cover.One of the latter was a Dornier Do 17Z, flying at 3,000 feet when spotted by red section of 253 Squadron led by Flight Lieutenant Raymond Duke-Woolley. Part of his combat report read: 'When at 10,000 feet near Beachy Head, Red 1 was advised that one enemy aircraft was approaching Dungeness at 3,000 feet. Section patrolled Beachy Head/Dungeness and observed one Dornier Do 17Z flying north in and out of the cloud at 3,000 feet. Section attacked in rotation from out of the sun, and enemy aircraft was seen to dive vertically into the ground three miles north of Newhaven.' It crashed at Tarring Neville.

During the late afternoon 302 (Polish)Squadron arrived with their British commanding officer, Squadron Leader Jack Satchell, to share the Westhampnett airfield with 602. A nearby field was now well endowed with a motley collection of tents, some of which collapsed under the weight of rainwater.

It was about this time that John Willie Hopkin put on a less than expert display for the new Polish pilots. Coming into land, he made a bad misjudgement and landed on Sandy Johnstone's Spitfire, which had been parked outside his office - writing off both aircraft. Sandy could be heard expressing his displeasure from some distance away, but the error didn't stop John Willie's career development, as he was made a flight commander early in 1941.

The squadron was brought to attention when the new chief of Fighter Command, Air Marshal Sir Sholto Douglas visited them: he had recently taken over from 'Stuffy' Dowding. Dowding had sent a farewell addressed to every pilot of Fighter Command:

'My Dear Fighter Boys,

In sending you this, my last message, I wish I could say all that is in my heart. I cannot hope to surpass the simple eloquence of the Prime Minister's words "Never in the field of human conflict was so much owed by so many to so few." That debt remains, and will increase.

In saying goodbye to you I want you to know how continually you have been in my thoughts, and that although direct connections may be severed, I may yet be able to help you in your gallant fight.

Goodbye to you, and God bless you all.'

During the early part of the afternoon, and halfway through the visit, the

Warts and All . . .

Towards the end of the Battle of Britain, the official war artist Cuthbert Orde arrived at Westhampnett, commissioned by the Air Ministry to sketch some of the more senior pilots of 602. Sandy Johnstone, Donald Jack, Findlay Boyd, Andy McDowall and Mickey Mount were selected.

The news got around the airfield like greased lightning, and very soon the wags were enjoying the vast amount of mickey taking that went on. As each pilot settled in the chair he had to undergo a volley of remarks such as 'See if he can draw in some hair for you Findlay' - for Boyd was fast losing his.

Then it was Donald Jack's turn. He was rather on the tall side: 'Can't see why they picked on you Donald, the canvas will only come up to your neck. Well, maybe that's for the best.'

Whereas Orde drew black and white sketches, a war artist specialising in oils, Olive Snell, also visited the airfield. Mickey

Clockwise, from top left: F/Lt Findlay Boyd, DFC and Bar; S/Ldr Sandy Johnstone, DFC; F/Lt Donald Jack; and F/Lt Mickey Mount, DFC.

Mount was again chosen, and he had to endure long sittings, accompanied by a barrage of jibes, taunts and rude remarks from his colleagues.

The drawings were free for the chosen few, but any of the lower ranked pilots, pilot officers and sergeants who wanted a drawing of themselves had to pay. The cost was £5, which in 1940 was a considerable amount of money: a pilot officer's weekly wage was around £4, a sergeant pilot's somewhat less. Out of the pilot's wages certain costs were levied. There were mess bills (a shilling for breakfast, 1s 6d each for dinner and supper), laundry bills and sports subscriptions - though what sports could have been played at Westhampnett, God only knows.

squadron was scrambled and was led off by Mickey Mount to face a number of enemy aircraft crossing the Channel and approaching the Isle of Wight. 213 Squadron were also scrambled to meet the incoming enemy force.

Helmut Wick, one of Germany's top Aces, led the incoming German force from JG 2 'Richthofen' Gerschwader. Keeping high, they were able to 'bounce' the British pilots. A desperate battle was soon in progress, with bullets flying and aircraft criss-crossing the sky, and Pat Lyall's Spitfire was hit. The other pilots taking part said that he seemed to have it under control as he went down. He was heading for a reasonable landing when it appeared that he suddenly decided to bale out at around 1,000 feet: he was seen to hit the ground before his parachute opened.

The Germans returned to their base, but Helmut Wick's 109s were soon refuelled and rearmed and back in the sky, heading for England once again. They took the same route, heading for Southampton. Two Squadrons, 152 and 609, were vectored to intercept. Wick's aircraft were flying at a higher altitude than the British fighters and they took full advantage, diving down at speed and catching the British pilots by surprise. Wick opened up and with his first shot brought down one of the Spitfires - his 56th combat

Pat Lyall: killed by the German Ace Helmut Wick.

victory. F/Lt John Dundas of 609 Squadron attacked Wick's Bf 109 and shot it down. He baled out, and his parachute was last seen south of the Needles. His wingman, Oberleutnant Rudi Pflanz, avenged the loss of his leader by shooting down John Dundas's Spitfire south of Bournemouth. His body was never found.

November turned into December, the last month of a momentous year. On December 8 the squadron was 'stood down' - the first time that this had occurred since it had been based at Westhampnett - so that everyone might attend the funeral of Pat Lyall. It was held during the afternoon at Brighton Crematorium.

The squadron's days at Westhampnett were now swiftly coming to a close. During the night of December 9 only one enemy reconnaissance flight was plotted over the south coast. The Luftwaffe paid no visit, but the RAF sent out 39 aircraft to attack German targets. Was this the turning point?

On December 12 Sandy Johnstone came back from a spot of leave, and when he arrived at Westhampnett he found that the squadron had been scrambled about half an hour before his arrival. Enemy aircraft had been plotted approaching the Kent coast. The squadron were successful in their interception, but lost one of their Spitfires. Jake Edy was the target of a Bf109 pilot, and he was very fortunate not to be killed. His aircraft had a large chunk of one its main planes shot away during the combat, and the rest parted company with the fuselage when he crashed into a flock of sheep grazing in a field near Folkestone, with Edy suffering minor injuries.

On arrival back at Westhampnett the squadron was greeted with the news that it was being rested, at last, and would be moving to Prestwick on Saturday. The news was greeted with mixed feelings by the pilots, as few of them had actually come from Scotland. Many of their predecessors had been posted elsewhere or had been killed or wounded. For the ground crews it was great news: they were nearly all from Scotland, and they were highly delighted at the thought of spending Christmas at home.

Saturday arrived and Westhampnett was a quagmire. The ground crews had already left for their long journey back to Scotland, but two days later the Spitfires were still on the ground, standing in the pouring rain while the pilots cursed their luck in the dispersal hut.

It ended in farce. On the 16th the squadron was ordered to return by train, leaving the Spitfires behind. The buses arrived to take them to the railway station, and they were soon loaded and on their way, but they were not destined to get very far. The police stopped hem near Midhurst and handed Sandy Johnstone sealed new orders. The pilots were instructed to return to Westhampnett, because the weather forecast indicated that it would be clear for flying the following day.

And so it was. With a stiff breeze blowing from the south, 602 Squadron set off for Scotland and, maybe, for adventures new.

Almost over: a photograph taken outside the officers' mess at Westhampnett in November, 1940. Seated, left to right, are F/l Mount DFC, F/l Boyd DFC, S/Ldr. Commanding Officer Sandy Johnstone DFC and Bar, S/Ldr Dunlop Urie and F/l Donald Jack. P/o Glen 'Nuts' Niven stands at the extreme right, with Paddy Barthrop sixth from the right.

The Squadron in 1941 and onwards

A rather funny thing happened to the squadron on its way back north. Sandy Johnstone had contacted Catterick on the way, asking permission for his twelve Spitfires to land and be refuelled. He was more than surprised when this permission was granted by its commanding officer.

The airfield soon came into sight, and when the pilots left their aircraft the petrol bowsers were soon at work. More surprising were the vehicles that quickly appeared to take the pilots to lunch – something they hadn't asked for or expected. Although Sandy thought it rather strange, he said nothing as he led his pilots into the mess.

A lovely lunch was spread out before them, laid as if they had been expected. The pilots tucked into a hearty lunch served by the mess stewards, and just as they were finishing their coffee they heard a huge roar outside. It was the distinctive sound of Merlin engines.

On hearing the noise one of the stewards came over to Sandy and inquired, 'You are 603 Squadron, aren't you?' Oh dear, what a mistake had been made!

As they left and headed for their aircraft 'Uncle' George Denholm the C.O. was coming in with 603 Squadron for whom the lunch had been ordered.

As you can imagine, 602 left with huge smiles on their faces when they realised the lunch hadn't been for them.

The squadron was now based at Prestwick on the western side of Scotland, a really cold place in winter, and on 13th March, 194, they were in action during attacks on Clydeside.

On 15th April, however, they were on the move yet again – to Heathfield, a new satellite airfield for Prestwick. In May they experienced action during more attacks on Clydeside, and around this time 'Sandy' Johnstone moved on, handing the reins over to Johnny Kilmartin. They were then swiftly passed on again – first to Pat Meagher, in June, and then to the famous Al Deere in August. It was the sort of shuffling around which could well upset the running of a squadron.

On the 10th May 1941, the German deputy fuhrer, Rudolf Hess, made a futile attempt to negotiate a peace treaty with the Duke of Hamilton. Piloting an ME110, he parachuted out near Eaglesham, leaving the aircraft to crash. The former 602 Battle of Britain pilot Hector MacLean was in the control room during this strange event.

Air and ground crews of 602 Squadron at Detling in March, 1944. The picture includes Max Sutherland and Pierre Clostermann, in the cockpit. [602 Sqadron Museum]

Bombs being backed onto the new Spitfires ready for Operation Big Ben, attacking V2 sites in Holland. [602 Squadron Museum]

A month after taking over, Al Deere led the squadron down south to Kenley. This was the start of attacking rather than defensive tactics. They were engaged in fighter sweeps across the Channel. These were 'circuses', or 'Rodeos', with more than two hundred aircraft. 'Ramrods' were the bomber escorts, and there were also 'Roadsteads' – attacks on coastal shipping – and 'Rhubarbs,' which were the low-level sorties by a small number of aircraft.

By this time there were few of the original auxiliaries still with the squadron. In July 1942 they moved to Peterhead, and then rather briefly back south in order to provide cover for the Dieppe Raid, during which they shot down five enemy aircraft.

In September 1942 the squadron was split into 'A' Flight and 'B' flight, moving to Skeabrae in the Orkneys and Sumburgh in the Shetlands respectively. There had been yet more changes in command – first Paddy Finucane and then Squadron Leader Peter Brothers. (The Squadron somehow seemed to attract the top stars to lead them.) Around this time 602 started to use the high altitude Spitfire VIs in order to intercept the high-flying enemy aircraft who were out on reconnaissance missions over Scapa Flow. After a few more trips down south from early January 1943, the squadron were engaged mostly on shipping escort duties and more offensive sweeps over France.

Another big star to lead the Squadron was Max Sutherland, when 602 returned to Skeabrae in February 1944. The war was gradually coming to its successful close, but there was still a lot of work to be done by the 'Boys of 602.'

The squadron was now equipped with Spitfire VII's – the 'Stratospits', which were used to great advantage. Ian Blair downed a high-flying ME109G on the 20th February. The other Spitfire Vs were described as 'clipped, clapped and cropped', not a patch on the Mark IX they had previously. By this time 602 had been joined by a number of Allied and Commonwealth pilots, including the Free French contingent – among them Pierre Clostermann, who tells his story in his book *Big Show*.

From the Orkneys they moved to Llanbedre in March 1944 with Spitfire 1X's to be fitted experimentally with 500-pound bombs. This was to attack the German 'flying bomb' sites, mainly situated in Holland.

Although 602 didn't know it, D-Day was being prepared, and in April 602 they found themselves based at Ford in West Sussex, close to their Westhampnett base during the 'Battle of Britain' almost four years earlier.

They continued their sweeps across the Channel, attacking various installations but in reality were getting ready for the invasion on the 6th June. That day dawned with bad weather, but 602 were up giving good cover to the landing crafts that were taking part.

A little later that month they were based in northern France, carrying out strafing attacks and ground attacks on just about anything that moved. By this time there was yet another change in command. The South African born Chris Le Roux, who had just taken over, was killed on 7th July and 'The Boss,' Max Sutherland, returned to take charge once again.

In September 1944 the squadron returned to England and were based at Coltishall, and they next moved on to Matlaske, where they were re-equipped with Mark XVIs for more concentrated attacks on the V2 flying bomb sites.

These attacks were code-named 'Big Ben' missions. The first one took place on Ist December on a site near the Royal Palace in The Hague. Such operations continued well into 1945, after the squadron had transferred to another base at Ludham.

On the 18th March 1945 Max Sutherland led a daring low-level attack on a Shell Mex building in The Hague which housed a variety of German personnel and was the headquarters of the V2 operation. There is no doubt that this was a dangerous and very daring raid and could only be carried out by pilots of the top quality. The height of the attack was barely above the chimney pots, and left

Above and below: Two stills from the film 'A Yank in the RAF', filwed with 602 Squadron's aircraft at Prestwick. [602 Squadron Museum]

them open to many means of attack by the enemy. There was no point in asking for volunteers for this dangerous mission: every pilot would have put his hand up, and Max Sutherland knew it. This was going to be a very spectacular mission – if it was successful.

Sutherland's wingman for this mission was Raymond Baxter (later of TV fame). 'Bax', as he was known, had to 'jink' in order to clear a church steeple. Flying in tight formation, he was unable to change position. 'All I could do,' he said afterwards, 'was to shut my eyes and blink.' Luckily, he cleared the steeple, and the attack was a roaring success.

By this time the war was coming to its conclusion, and – although they didn't know it – so was 602 Squadron. It was disbanded in May 1945 after a long and distinguished life, and after once more giving a great account of themselves.

The end of the story? Not so. As we shall see, within thirteen months the squadron would rise again.

602 Squadron pilots seen in front of a Spitfire LF XVIE shortly before the squadron disbanded at Coltishall in May, 1945. [602 Squadron Museum]

602 Squadron Commanding Officers

Squadron Leader C. N. Lowe MC DFC   (September 1925–January 1926)
Captain J.D. Latta MC   (February 1926–May 1927)
Squadron Leader J. Fullerton.   (May 1927–May 1932)
The Marquess of Douglas and Clydesdale AFC   (May 1932–September 1936)
Squadron Leader D.F. MacIntyre AFC   (September 1936–October 1937)
Squadron Leader A. D. Farquhar DFC   (October 1937–April 1940)
Squadron Leader Geo. C. Pinkerton OBE DFC   (April 1940–July 1940)
Squadron Leader A.V.R. Johnstone DFC   (July 1940–April 1941)
Squadron Leader J. I. Kilmartin OBE DFC   (April 1941–June 1941)
Squadron Leader P. Meagher DSO DFC   (June 1941–August 1941)
Squadron Leader A. C. Deere DSO OBE DFC   (August 1941–January 1942)
Squadron Leader 'Paddy' Finucane DSO DFC   (January 1942–June 1942)
Squadron Leader P. M. Brothers DSO DFC   (June 1942–October 1942)
Squadron Leader M.F. Beytagh DFC   (October 1942–October 1943)
Squadron Leader 'Max' Sutherland DFC   (October 1943–July 1944)
Squadron Leader 'Chris' Le Roux DFC   (July 1944–August 1944 – KIA)
Flight Lieutenant A.R. Stewart Temp   (August 1944)
Squadron Leader 'Max' Sutherland DFC   (August 1944–May 1945)
Squadron Leader Marcus Robinson AFC   September 1946–August 1950)
Squadron Leader H.M.Stephen DSO DFC   (September 1950–July 1952)
Squadron Leader J. A. Forrest   (July 1952–October 1953)
Squadron Leader R. B. Davidson DFC   (October 1953–May 1956)
Squadron Leader C. D. Bartman   (May 1956–March 1957)
Squadron Leader G. Lyall AE   (from July 2006)

KIA – Killed in Action

*Peter Brothers DSO, DFC
reading a report from one
of his flight leaders.
Brothers commanded
602 from June to October,
1942. [Author's
collection]*

602 Reformed

As a result of a decision by the Air Ministry to reform auxiliary squadrons, 602 were reformed on 11th June 1946 and based at RNAS Abbotsinch, with Squadron Leader Marcus Robinson AFC as commander. He was probably the best choice to be in charge. He gladly dropped two ranks from group captain in order to take over the squadron. He wasn't the only one, as a number of men dropped ranks in order to join a very limited establishment as non-commissioned aircrew.

The first aircraft to be delivered to the squadron was a strange choice, a North American Harvard T.2 KF 374, and they had to wait almost four months before the first Spitfire was delivered – an FR 14e TP236 and coded as RAI-A.

In the aftermath of the war the country faced huge economic problems, and the social life of the population struggled to adjust. Quite a few of the post war members were keen to re-join, and these included such people as sergeants McKinnon and Harry Henderson, who had been with 602 in 1931. The padre, Rev Lewis Sutherland (another pre-war stalwart) resumed his duties of looking after the 602 flock, which included seeing the lads off playing their famous bagpipes.

Another stalwart also re-joined: the civilian admin officer Glen 'Nuts' Niven. He was a man who just couldn't keep away. He was affectionately known as 'Mr. 602' and he was proud of that title – a wonderful man who strongly believed that a spade was a spade.

Jack Daly, Glen 'Nuts' Niven and Jim Johnston. Glen was a wonderful man. I corresponded with him for many years and had the privilege of meeting him at his home in Glasgow in 2000. [602 Squadron Museum]

During 1947 the squadron received Spitfire 2Is as its operational type and, in addition, a few Mark 14s for training. The big, heavy machines were quite a handful — 'the wings wanted to go around the engine'. Sadly two accidents occurred, with Ivor Reid (during the first camp at Woodvale in July 1947) and Hamish McWilliam, in April 1948, both losing their lives.

Jim Johnston DFC managed to walk away from a very skilled force landing near GlenBoig on 31st October 1948 and, yet again, at the 1949 annual camp at Horsham St. Faith in what is now Glasgow's Spitfire LA198. During that camp the squadron had celebrated the 40th anniversary of Bleriot's Channel crossing at Torquet – Jack Forrest giving a post prandial 'demonstration tres Dangereux'.

In January 1951 the 'whine and whistle' of the Goblin became very familiar over Clydeside as the squadron was re-equipped with DeHavilland Vampires plus two Meteor T7s for instrument training and jet familiarisation, there being no two seat Vampires at that time. The squadron moved back to their old home at Renfrew while proper runways were laid at Abbotsinch. It did eventually get a Vampire T.11 – a few weeks before disbandment.

The 'Kiddy-car', as it was known, was much appreciated and they soon began to sport the famous 602 markings, the Grey Douglas tartan together with the reinstated 'LO' code letters in place of the Reserve Command 'RAI' markings – the auxiliaries having been transferred back to Fighter Command in November 1949.

Enter the jet age. Vampires of 602 pictured in January, 1951. The aircraft have been lined up for a press call. [602 Squadron Museum]

In September 1950 there was a change in command when Harborne Stephen DSO DFC became the commanding officer. He was a newspaper executive with a very distinguished war record. He, in turn, was replaced by Jack Forrest in July 1952. Jack was to be the last auxiliary to command the Squadron – until 2006.

Associated with the Fighter Squadron, post war, were 2602 RAF Regiment Squadron (Light Anti-Aircraft) and 3602 (Fighter Control Unit), both based at RAF Bishopbriggs.

It was the Korean war emergency that prompted the mobilisation of the auxiliaries. On 15th April 1951, 602 personnel were called up and moved to Leuchars for a period of continuous training along side the regulars. The 603 and 612 Squadrons used the time there to convert to Vampires. The three Scottish auxiliaries would thereafter occasionally engage together in a 'Wing-Ding.'

602 on parade. Sqd Leader Marcus Robinson AFC leads the march past in Glasgow in November, 1949.
[602 Squadron Museum]

During a visit to the 602 Squadron, the C-in-C Fighter Command, Air Marshall Sir Basil Embrey, was giving the squadron a 'pep-talk', and Jack Daly celebrated the occasion by just having a 'flame-out'. He pulled off a successful forced landing on the airfield, though having hit a raised concrete coping. The Vampire however was a write off.

Business pressures forced Jack Forrest to relinquish his command of 602 and then, in October 1953, a regular officer – Bert Davidson – came in to take over. Sadly the spacious pre-war days were over.

It is noted in the ORB for January 1954 that 'seven aircraft were airborne over Glasgow,' the first time for many months that a formation of any size was able to display its talents to the Glaswegians.

November 1955 was billed as one of the worst winter months for some years when just twelve days of flying were possible. However, 602 managed to get what were named affectionately as 'Rats and Terriers' exercises. It appears that one aircraft must fire inverted from 90 degrees off to get an 'A' rating on cine film these days. However, to prove their wonderful capabilities they won the coveted 'Cooper Trophy' for the most improved Squadron in 1956 – a wonderful achievement to add to the many they had already received.

The squadron were excited when they heard that they were to have their Vampires replaced by Hawker Hunters, but this was not to be. In fact the news

602 Squadron Bases

Renfrew	(September 1925.)
Abbotsinch	(January 1933.)
Grangemouth	(October 1939.)
Drem	(October 1939.)
Montrose and Dyce	(April 1940.)
Drem	(May 1940.)
Westhampnet	(August 1940.)
Prestwick	(December 1940.)
Ayr (Heathfield)	(April 1941.)
Kenley	(July 1941.)
Redhill	(January 1942.)
Kenley	(March 1942.)
Redhill	(May 1942.)
Peterhead	July 1942.)
Skeabrae&Sumburgh	(September 1942)
Perranporth	(January 1943.)
Lasham	(April 1943.)
Fairlop	(April 1943.)
Bognor	(June 1943.)
Kingsnorth	(July 1943.)
Newchurch	(August 1943.)
Detling	(October 1943.)
Skeabrae	(January 1944.)
Detling	(March 1944.)
Llanbedr	(March 1944.)
Detling	(March 1944.)
Ford	(April 1944.)
B11 Longues	(June 1944.)
B19 Lingevres	(August 1944.)
B40 Nivillers	(September 1944.)
B70 Deurne	(September 1944.)
Coltishall	(September 1944.)
Matlaske	(October 1944.)
Ludham	(February 1945.)
Coltishall	(April 1945 Disbanded May 1945.)
Abbotsinch	(Reformed June 1946.)
Renfrew	(June 1949.)
Abbotsinch	(June 1954. – Disbanded in March 1957.)

was much worse. It was announced in January 1957 that all the flying squadrons of the Royal Auxiliary Air Force were to be disbanded by 10th March.

The squadron was devastated once more. In addition to this bad news, 602's compatriots at Abbotsinch – numbers 1830 and 1843 Squadrons, The Scottish Air Division, RNVR and 1967 Flight of number 666 Air Observation Post Squadron – would also be disbanded. It didn't make any sense to the defences of this island for this to happen. HM Treasury ruled OK then, as it does now.

The final words in the squadron's ORB, written by the regular adjutant, Johnny Walker, were: 'Good feelings, not so good.'

The last parade was held at Abbotsinch on the 27th January and reviewed by the Duke of Hamilton. The Squadron Standard, awarded in 1952, was presented during the morning of the 3rd March and laid up in Glasgow Cathedral that afternoon.

The Famous 602 (City of Glasgow) Squadron was no more.

Cave leonem cruciatum.

Sqadron leader Don Bartman and his men bid farewell at Abbotsinch on Sunday 27th January, 1957. Note the rows of medals on these wonderful members of 602. [602 Squadron Museum]

The 602 (City of Glasgow) Squadron Museum

The 602 (City of Glasgow) Squadron Museum was founded in 1982 by the Training Corps Cadets of No. 2175 (Rolls Royce) Squadron under the leadership of the commanding officer, Flight Lieutenant Bill McConnel – the personnel manager of Rolls Royce in Glasgow.

The building was close to their HQ, situated on a former Avon jet engine site, adjacent to the company's Hillington facility.

The idea for a museum came about after the cadets were given wreckage from the 'Humbie' Heinkel 111, shot down by 602 Squadron on 28th October 1939. The first German aircraft to be brought down on British soil during WWII, it had landed more or less intact in the Humbie Hills just south of Edinburgh. The pieces of wreckage had lain in a corner of the factory for more than forty years.

Bill McConnell and the cadets in the 602 Squadron Museum at Hillington. They devised and built the museum – a truly magical place to visit.

The engine itself had been examined by Rolls Royce engineers in the early days. The cadets were very excited at receiving the wreckage, and it wasn't long before they hit on the idea of a museum dedicated to 602 Squadron.

Before they could start they were set the task of researching the squadron, and were surprised to find that in Glasgow there was nothing about its very own squadron. The seeds were sown: they decided there and then that people should know more about 602 and the people who served with it. They set about creating a custom-built museum, collecting anything and everything associated with the squadron, and they had soon collected a vast array of items. Such was their dedication and success that the Marshall of the Royal Air Force, the Lord Cameron of Balhouse, formally opened the museum in October 1983, to a fly-past of Phantoms of 43 Squadron based at RAF Leuchars.

Over the years the Museum Association membership has grown to around five hundred, a wonderful achievement. Run by a dedicated and active committee.

The Rolls Royce Hillington facility was built as a wartime shadow factory in 1939 for the production of Merlin Aero engines. However the wartime premises were now unsuitable for modern manufacture and the company moved to a state of the art facility at nearby Inchinnan with the resultant closure of the Hillington site and the consequential relocation of the 602 Squadron Museum. It is now to be found within the Royal Highland Fusiliers' Museum in Sauchiehall Street, Glasgow.

Note:
I recall flying up to Glasgow in 2000 and being met by a lovely man, Gordon Catto, who looked after me while I was there. I visited the old Hillington Museum for the 60th Anniversary of the Battle of Britain and met people who had taken part in that famous event. There were both aircrew and ground staff, who really never got the praise they fully deserved. Two people I met were Glen 'Nuts' Niven at his home and Donald Jack, both Battle of Britain pilots and just wonderful people. That is also when I met the current secretary, Roddy MacGregor, who – like the others – is an absolute charming gentleman.

602 (City of Glasgow) Squadron.
Roll of Honour

1939–1945

Sergeant B. P. Bailey
Sergeant H. E. Barton
Aircraftsman 1st Class R.W. Bishop
Sergeant C. A. Booty
Sergeant E. Brayley
Sergeant I. M. Brown
Sergeant W.L. Brown
Sergeant J.M.C. Bryden
F/Sergeant L.H. Chalice
Flying Officer W.H. Coverley
F/Lieutentant F. De Naeyer
Flying officer G.J. Drake
Sergeant D.W. Eelcome
Wing Commander B.E.F. Finucane
        DSO, DFC and 2 bars
Flying Officer M.W. Frith
Sergeant P.F. Green
Flying Officer D.R. Hale
Sergeant P.L. Hauser
Sergeant A.R. Hedger
Flying Officer G.S. Jones

Flying Officer J.W. Kelly
Sq. Leader J.J. Le Roux DFC – 2 bars
Flight Lieutenant G.Y.G. Lloyd
Pilot Officer A. Lyall
Flight Lieutenant P.A. Major
Pilot Officer H.W. Moody
Sergeant F.W. Morrell
Sergeasnt J.A. Nicholson
F/Sergeant J.D. O'Connor
Sergeant D.V. Osborne
Warrant Officer J.D. Pincus
Warrant Officer R. Ptacek
LAC. A. Richardson
Flight Lieutenant T.G.F. Ritchie
Sergeant S. Smith
Sergeant M.H. Sprague
Sergeant C.J. Squibb
Pilot Officer A.R. Tidman
Sergeant B.E.P. Whall DFM
Flying Officer J.C. Yates

We Will Always Remember Them

Appendix 1

The fate of a German bomber which attacked London at lunchtime on Battle of Britain Day, Sunday, 15th September 1940 (see page 89).

1/KG76. Dornier Do 17Z (Reg. No. 2361)

Pilot, Oberleutnant Robert Zehbe.
Rear gunner, Uffz. Gustav Hubel
Mechanic, Uffz. Leo Hammermeister
Observer, Uffz. Hans Goschenhofer
Wireless operator, Oberg. Ludwig Armbruster

Based at Nivelles, just south of Beauvais, the plane took off at 10.05am and joined the main formation over Cap Gris-Nez. They crossed the coast over Dungeness.

The Dornier was shot down at 11.50am after being attacked by no fewer than six fighter aircraft. The first attack was carried out by Flight Lieutenant Jeffries of 310 Squadron, followed by other pilots of his squadron. The final attack came from pilot sergeant Ray Holmes of 504 Squadron, who having expended all his ammunition manoeuvred his Hurricane and with his port wing struck the

Possibly the most iconic picture of World War II: the Dornier, minus parts of its wings and tail, crashes down on Victoria Station. [Author's collection]

Damage caused by the crashed Dornier at Victoria Railway Station, London, on Battle of Britain Day. [L. Standard]

The tail unit of the Dornier bomber on rooftops in Vauxhall Bridge Road.

Dornier's port tail section. The tail section came away with Hubel, the rear gunner, still inside it and crashed down to earth. Meanwhile the enemy aircraft was now spiralling out of control towards London and landed in the forecourt of Victoria railway station. The tail section, containing Hubel's body, landed on the roofs of buildings in Vauxhall Bridge Road.

The out-of-control aircraft was the subject of many photographs and became an iconic picture of the war.

Hubel and Goschenhofer were both killed in the action and were later buried at Cannock Chase. Hammermeister and Armbruster baled out at 3,000ft and were captured: Hammermeister was wounded in the action, landed near Dulwich and was taken to hospital; Armbruster came down in Wells Park Road, Sydenham.

The 27-year-old pilot, Oberleutnant Robert Zehbe, although badly wounded, managed to bale out of the doomed German aircraft and landed in the street in Kennington. His parachute was torn to shreds by a mob of local people who had quickly gathered, and who then turned on the pilot, causing him further serious injuries. He was rescued by the authorities and taken to hospital, where he died the following day. He was buried in Brookwood Military cemetery.

And another fragment: what looks the tail wheel of the Dornier at the corner of Wilton Road and Terminus Place, London. [L. Standard]

This aircraft and crew had taken part in the first daylight raid on London on 7th September as well as the low level attack on Kenley aerodrome on 18th August 1940.

Meanwhile Ray Holmes's Hurricane was also damaged during the collision with the Dornier and failed to respond to the controls. Holmes was forced to bale out and landed in Hugh Street, Chelsea. Meanwhile his Hurricane, no. 2725, crashed and burned out near Fountain Court, Buckingham Palace.

Raymond Tower Holmes, service no. 68730

He joined the RAFVR in February 1937 as an airman u/t pilot and began his flying training at Prestwick. He was commissioned in June 1941 He took part in many overseas operations and moved from Hurricanes to Spitfires.

He was further promoted to Flying Officer in June 1942 and to Flight lieutenant on 10th June 1943.

He became a King's messenger for Winston Churchill when he was preparing for the famous Potsdam Conference, flying mail between London and Biarritz, and between Berlin and London when he was at Potsdam.

He left the squadron at the end of August and was released from the RAF on October 4th 1945 as a Flight Lieutenant.

Appendix 2

Did a pilot from 602 Squadron shoot Rommel in 1944?

I have long held the belief that it was a pilot from 602 Squadron who shot up Field Marshal Rommel's staff car in Normandy on 17th July, 1944. Over the years I have endeavoured to find out which pilot it was. I have made numerous enquiries without a significant result. I have now enlisted the help of two people who have a detailed knowledge of this period of aviation history.

Even with their help, however, the picture has become even more confusing – with the possibility that it wasn't a 602 pilot after all.

In July 1944 602 Squadron were based at Longues and commanded by Chris Le Roux DFC. (The incident occurred about a month before he lost his life.) No pilot at that time could have known it was Rommel in the staff car that was hit. Indeed, it was only after the war that it transpired that Rommel had sustained serious injuries in the attack– and only then that the surviving passengers in Rommel's vehicle reported that they had been attacked by a Spitfire.

How certain can they have been? The main concern at the time was to try and evade the attacking aircraft and protect Rommel from any injuries. It would have been so easy to get the type of aircraft wrong. After all, it would have been travelling in excess of 200 miles per hour and their first sight of it was probably the front of it.

The RAF view is that the question 'Who shot up Rommel?' is in the same category as 'Who shot down the famous Red Baron?' Neither question has yet been satisfactorily answered.

Rommel in his official staff car, seen with his driver, Sergeant Daniel, who was killed in the attack in July, 1944.

No fewer than seven wartime pilots later claimed to have done the deed:

Sqn/Ldr J.J.Chris Le Roux of 602 Squadron.
Aspirant Jacques Reminger of 602 Squadron.
Flt/Lt. Charley Fox of 412 Squadron Royal Canadian Air Force.
Lt. R. Jenkins of USAAF
Flt/Lt. Switzer of 193 Squadron, RAF
Fg/Off. Stanski of 308 Squadron RAF. And
Flt.Lt. Baldwin of 609 Squadron, RAF

Many believe that it was Jacques Reminger who actually did shoot up Rommel's staff car. RAF form 540 shows that 602 Squadron landed at 16.45 hours. It is thought that Rommel was shot up around 1800 hours, but there is a possibility that the two sides were operating on different time scales. In any case, just how accurate are the combat reports?

I personally come down on the side of Jacques Reminger, not because I want to but because, as far as I can judge, I seriously think he has the best claim. What do you think?

On 17th July 1944 Rommel and a number of his staff had left their base and gone to the German headquarters on the front line. The Allied invasion was in

full swing, and massive gains had been achieved by the Allied troops since D-Day on 6th June. Hitler had been totally convinced that the allied invasion would come in the Calais area, a mere 22-mile trip across the Channel from Dover. The assumption was that the rest of France was too far from England. Rommel was not so sure, and on several occasions told Hitler this. History, of course, now proves that Rommel was correct.

When Rommel was first given the job in Normandy he was appalled at the poor defences. He had the Germans working day and night in an effort to strengthen these defences and build a formidable 'Atlantic Wall'. He visited the coastal area every day prior to D-Day to check for himself how the war was going and to issue encouragement to the troops.

Having completed his normal inspection, he began his return journey back to his headquarters at around 1600 hours. Since midday the allied aircraft had kept up an intense attack in the area and had strafed

Rommel on one of his many Atlantic Wall inspections – here in 1944, just before D-Day. [Author's collection]

many vehicles travelling along the French roads. Burnt out and burning vehicles littered the roads, with dead and wounded soldiers lying close by. Just before 1800 hours Rommel's car reached the outskirts of Livarot, having by then passed many of these stricken vehicles.

From roughly this point a tree-covered road descended from Livarot until it reached the highway some two and a half miles outside Vinoutiers. As Rommel's staff car drew nearer they could see about eight allied fighter bombers over Livarot. It turned out later that these were the ones observing and attacking traffic on these roads..

After a short discussion in the car it was decided that in their opinion these aircraft had not yet spotted them, and so with Rommel anxious to get back to his headquarters, they decided that they would continue their journey. The road here was straight between the two French towns, affording a good view for the driver.

Suddenly the air observer, Lance Corporal Karl Hulke, reported that two aircraft were closing in fast. The driver, Sergeant Daniel, quickly glanced over his shoulder and immediately accelerated to top speed, heading for a turning about 300 metres ahead of them. This led to a small track and would afford them some cover.

The vehicle had almost reached this turning when the aircraft attacked. As the leading plane came in, Rommel looked back and a burst of fire ripped along

The state funeral of Rommel, held in Ulm and organised by Hitler. Within months of surviving the air attack, he committed suicide by swallowing a cynanide capsule on the fuhrer's instructions. The German people weren't told the truth about his death.

the side of his vehicle. Sergeant Daniel was hit in the left shoulder and arm. Rommel was struck in the face by glass splinters and suffered a shrapnel wound in the left temple and cheekbone, causing a triple fracture of the skull which rendered him unconscious. Major Neuhaus, another passenger in the staff car was, also hit – a shell striking his pistol holster and subsequently causing a fractured pelvis.

Sergeant Daniel's injuries were so severe that he lost control of the speeding staff car. It struck a tree stump on the right-hand side of the road and ended up embedded at a sharp angle on the other side.

Rommel who had been sitting in the right-hand jump seat when the attack began, was thrown from the vehicle by the force of the crash and lay on the roadside some 66ft behind the car.

Captain Lang, Rommel's staff officer, and corporal Holke both managed to jump clear of the vehicle and run for cover by the roadside. The second aircraft now flew back over the crash site and fired at the wounded men lying on the ground. Rommel lay by the roadside unconscious, splattered with blood and bleeding profusely from his facial injuries – from his eyes and mouth in particular. He had apparently been hit in the left temple. Rommel was still unconscious when help arrived.

Conveyed to a local military hospital, he was eventually discharged and went home to continue his recovery. Within three months, however, he would be dead – not from his injuries but after swallowing a cyanide capsule.

Corporal Karl Hulke, the air sentry, said later, 'When I realised that there were two bombers about to attack us. I told Captain Lang and the field marshal (Rommel) of course. I was in such a state I screamed. It all happened so quickly – they shot at us.'

And Jacques Reminger's memory of the event?

'We took off,' he reported, 'our orders being to stop any vehicles we saw moving. We were to shoot anything moving on the roads and approaching Livarot towards any of the towns such as Vinoutiers. This was the centre of this operation. About 6pm we spotted an open-top staff car on the road driving towards Livoutiers.

'For us we were just shooting at a vehicle, a staff car. I hit the staff car. It was on its own and not in a convoy. Who was in it, I don't know. To me it was just a target – we didn't have time to exchange visiting cards at 400 miles per hour. It was only after the war that I found out who was in the car.'

Right: General Burgdorf, Hitler's adjutant, who brought the potassium cyanide capsule to Rommel at his home. Rommel died soon after swallowing it.

Below: Rommel's house in Herrlingen under close surveillance by the Gestapo.

Appendix 3

Two 602 Squadron combat reports for August 1940.

F.C.C.R./481/40   S E C R E T

FORM "F"

FIGHTER COMMAND COMBAT REPORT

--+-------------------- --------------- ------------------------------------

TO :-   H.Q. FIGHTER COMMAND.

FROM :-   H.Q. 11 GROUP.

INTELLIGENCE PATROL REPORT, No. 602 Squadron 16.8.40.

    Combats took place 6 miles North of Worthing and also North of Arundel 5,000 feet approximately at 1655 hours and 1710 hours.

    Blue Section of four Spitfires took off West of Hampnett 1629 hours to patrol base 15,000 feet. Vectored Eastwards below clouds (which were 7,000 feet) and over Worthing sighted a single He.111 flying Northwards. All a/c of Blue Section attacked from above, beam and astern attacks being employed. E/A took no evasive action; return fire was experienced from stern gunner and one Spitfire was hit but not rendered unserviceable.

    Returing to base at 1710 hours, one Me.110 sighted 1000 feet flying North. Blue 2 climbed onto tail; opened fire 100 yards closing to 50 feet. Saw e/a crash. No evasive action was taken and return fire of e/a did not strike Spitfire. Section landed 1745 hours.

    Total rounds fired :-   10080
    No. cine gun.   No. A.A. fire.

Own Casualties :- NIL.
Enemy Casualties :- 1 Me.110 destroyed.
              1 He.111 destroyed.

                    Signed,
                        O.H. Cranebrook,
                          Intelligence Officer,
                          No. 602 Squadron.

FC/S.17570 /INT.
9.9.40.

FCCR/590/40.

FIGHTER COMMAND COMBAT REPORT

TO: HEADQUARTERS, FIGHTER COMMAND.

FROM: NO. 11 GROUP INTELLIGENCE

INTELLIGENCE PATROL REPORT
602 Squadron - 26.8.40.

Combat took place over Selsey Bill 15.25 hrs. at 15,000 ft. 11 Spitfires, 602 Squadron, took off W.Hampnett at 16.13 hours, ordered to intercept a large number of e/a approaching Portsmouth. When at 14,000 feet about 150 e/a were sighted approaching from 10 miles South, and Squadron climbed to 17,000 feet S.W. to get above in sun. Squadron then attacked, and as they attacked, enemy formation was seen to split into two, one part making off S.E. and the other S.W. E/a attacked by Spitfires were part that turned S.W. About 100 escorting Me.109s were seen 3,000 feet above and several miles astern on port quarter of bombers. Red Leader, (S/Ldr.A.V.R. Johnstone) reports: "...From experience, I did not think enemy fighters would come down even to protect bombers; I therefore ordered Squadron to attack bombers in line astern". Red 1 and Red 2 attacked bombers and disarranged their formation, experiencing heavy cross fire. Red 1 attacked one He.111 astern and above and a second astern below; bursts 5 sec. from 1,000 yards closing to 150 yards, and 3 sec. opening 400 yards closing to 200 yds., claiming latter damaged. It was subsequently attacked by Hurricanes. Red 2 attacked outside left He.111, full beam, 8 sec. opening 300 yds. closing to 75 yards, and again full beam, 4 sec. opening 200 yards, closing to 100 yards. This E/a crashed and was burnt out in marshes W. of Pagham. Red 3 attacked same E/a as Red 1, full beam, full astern and quarter, 3 attacks of 2 sec. each, saw E/a glide down with one engine stopped before Hurricanes attacked. Believed to have landed near Ford. Yellow 2 attacked a Do.17 or 215 astern above, 4 sec. opening 300 yards, closing to 50 yards, and saw a lot of white smoke come from port engine. He then attacked Do.17 which was separated, quarter below, 6 secs. 200 yards, closing to 50 yards, and saw fire break out in fuselage by wing stub. Police confirm that this e/a crashed in sea 3 miles S. of Pagham.
Blue 1 attacked a single Heinkel with no result observed. He then attacked a formation of 15 Heinkels in 3 vics of 5, firing at four and putting one motor of one of them out of action.
Green 3, after attacking 2 Me.109s without effect, attacked a He.111 on flank of E/a formation, full beam from above, 2 sec. opening 250 yards, closing to 100 yards, and four more short bursts and saw e/a land in flames on beach at W.Wittering.
Blue 3 then chased a He.111 out to sea, attacked quarter to starboard, 3 sec. opening 250 yards closing to 100 yards, and again quarter to port 3 sec. 250 yds. to 100 yds. saw e/a on fire in sea.

Weather - Visibility 20 miles, cloud 7,000 ft. 5/10ths.
Fire of Me.109s reported as very wild.
Total ammunition - 13,500 rounds, one stoppage due to
                        separated case.
Seven Spitfires landed W.Hampnett by 17.10 hours.
Enemy losses - 3 He.111 destroyed.
               1 Do.17 destroyed.
OUR losses - F/O.McLean seriously wounded in foot.
             2 Spitfires written off.

(sd) for F/O.Grazebrook
E.A.Dennis F/Lt.

My thanks

No book is finished without a few words of thanks to those who have helped me in the production of it. The original 'Spitfires over Sussex' took close on four years of research and writing, and as a result there were many people who deserved my thanks for the help and co-operation afforded to me over the initial period. It was also the first book I had written and published under my own imprint. My initial thanks were directed at a number of what I would describe as '602 stars,' including Glen Niven, Sandy Johnstone, Donald Jack and 'Paddy' Barthropp – sadly all now passed on to a higher place in the skies. There was also Douglas McRoberts, author of the wonderful book *Lions Rampant*, and who is now the Reverend Douglas McRoberts.

I mustn't forget Gordon Catto, who looked after me when I spent a wonderful weekend in Glasgow in 2000, when the 60th anniversary of the Battle of Britain was celebrated at the 602 Museum. He enlightened me on many interesting things about the squadron. All these people answered my letters with some great detail.

Several other people who have greatly assisted me with the new part of this book. These include Roddy MacGregor, who has spent many hours finding and sending me a number of very interesting documents from the 602 (City of Glasgow) Squadron Museum. My thanks, too, to Mr. Gerry Traynor, the 602 historian. I am most grateful to him for pointing out a number of errors in my initial scripts. I must also includehere Iain Sutherland who has recently passed away.

Dugald Cameron OBE DSc, a brilliant artist, assisted me with my initial 602 book some 10 years ago. Together with Mr. Alan Carlaw he has produced *No. 602 (City of Glasgow) Squadron, Reformation of Squadron – 1st July 2006*, a book full of wonderful pictures and illuminating text.

Over the past 10 or so years I have been able to correspond with some wonderful people, including Roddy MacGregor, Gordon Catto, Glen Niven and Donald Jack. They have each helped me with my research in so many different ways, and I shall always be indebted to them.

I can't conclude this note of thanks without mentioning my wife Christine who allows me to make a mess at home and to get away with it; Elliot, my grandson and a lovely lad who is getting better and better with his IT work; and my editor, David Arscott, who sorts out the mess I call a book and actually makes it into something worthwhile.

My grateful thanks to them all.

Telscombe Cliffs 2010

Bibliography

Aces High, Christopher Shores and Clive Williams (Grub Street, London).

Adventure in the Sky, Sandy Johnstone (William Kimber, London)

Battle of Britain, The, Len Deighton (Book Club Associates / Jonathan Cape).

Battle of Britain, The, Richard Townsend Bickers (Salamander Books, London).

Battle of Britain, The, Now and Then, ed. William Ramsey (Battle of Britain Prints International, London)

Enemy in the Sky, 'Sandy' Johnstone (William Kimber, London)

Fighters in Defence, Hector MacLean (Squadron Prints, Glasgow).

Flying Scots, The, Jack Webster (Glagow Royal Concert Hall).

Glasgow's Fighter Squadron, Fred G. Nancarrow (Collins Clear Type Press, London & Glasgow).

Glasgow's Own, Dugald Cameron (Squadron Prints, Glasgow)

JG 26 War Diary, The, vol. one: 1939-1942, Donald Caldwell (Grub Street, London).

Lions Rampant, Douglas McRoberts (William Kimber, London).

Men of the Battle of Britain, Kenneth G. Wynn (CCB Associates, South Croydon).

The Narrow Margin, Derek Wood and Derek Dempster (Arrow Books, London).

Paddy, The life and times of, Patrick Barthropp(Howard Baker Press, London).

Scramble, a narrative history of the Battle of Britain, Norman Gelb (Michael Joseph, London).

Spitfire into War, Sandy Johnstone (Grafton Books, London)

Index of People

see also 'Roll of honour', p 142